NEW PSYCHOANALYTIC DIMENSIONS:
FROM THE INDIVIDUAL TO THE INSTITUTIONS

Henrique Guilherme Scatolin

2nd Edition

USA – 2016

NEW PSYCHOANALYTIC DIMENSIONS
By SCATOLIN, Henrique—2nd ed. — 2016
1st Edition Published by David Publishing LLC
Includes bibliographical references and index
ISBN: 978-1-943350-53-7
1. Psychology — Freudian theory
2. Psychology— Movements
3. Psychology — Psychoanalysis

GlobalSouth
PRESS

Bulent Acma, Ph.D.
Department of Economics, Anadolu University, Eskişehir, Turkey.

Flavio Saraiva, Ph.D.
Universidade Nacional de Brasília, Brasilia, Brazil.

Helmunt Schlenter, Ph.D.
Institute for Global Dialogue, Pretoria, South Africa.

Tullo Vigevani, Ph.D.
Sao Paulo State University, Sao Paulo, Brazil.

Monica Arruda Almeida, Ph. D.
Georgetown University, Washington, D.C., United States of America.

Yong J. Wang, Ph.D.
Ohio University, Columbus, United States of America.

Chih-yu Shih, Ph.D.
National Taiwan University (ROC), Taipei, Taiwan.

Irene Klumbies, Ph.D.
Jacobs University Bremen, Bremen, Germany.

Sai Felicia Krishna-Hensel, Ph.D.
Center Business and Econ. Develop., Auburn University at Montgomery, Montgomery, United States of America.

José Álvaro Moisés, Ph.D.
Universidade de São Paulo (USP), São Paulo, Brazil

Summary

Presentation

In a conjuncture in which psychoanalysis persists and resists the criticism of a paralyzed academy, the book **New Psychoanalytic Dimensions: from the individual to the institutions** comes to provide the reader a new perspective of human uniqueness, from the micro level to the meso level. But what is there in this book that comes to whet the reading of young readers? So, to answer this question, we will make a little tour from the individual (micro) to the institutional (meso).

When I refer to the micro level in this book, I am alluding, in a first moment, to the male psychic constitution in the Freudian work, a moment in which I resume the core concepts in the Sigmund Freud work for the understanding of the male uniqueness and subjectivity.

Meanwhile, I bring from the French psychoanalyst Piera Aulagnier the postulates of the originary, primary and secondary for understanding the psychic constitution, punctuating this book from the discussion of the "I" constitution. Although she is a psychoanalyst impregnated by the Lacanian conception, Aulagnier brings a unique legacy in her conception of the originary concept, a process in which precedes the primary of the Freudian theory. But what is there in this process only a reading of her contributions, present in this book, can reply it.

Still in the micro or individual level, this book discusses the characteristics of obsessional neurosis present in the 'ruminant' thought of the obsessive. For this purpose, it focuses on the archaic forms of this thought, such as animism and defense mechanisms that lies in the uniqueness of this neurosis, making the obsessional thought analogous to the most remote infantile desires. Thus, the obsessive thinks, thinks, and thinks, but now of acting, he is invaded by his uncertainties.

And these are the uncertainties, the ambivalences and the entire dynamics of the sadistic-anal fixation, determinant of the obsessional symptomatology, which will be resumed in a singular analysis of a clinical case present at the chapter dedicated to ambivalent manifestations of the neurotic symptom. In this chapter I dedicate a special attention to the anal-sadistic phase interconnected to the doubt symptom. What do both have in common? All or nothing?

And in the intricacies of Freudian neurosis, by another bias, I bring the famous conversion hysteria or the hysteria itself, not in a clinical case, but rather through contemporary reflections from the phallic logic and the symptomatic positivity. If, in obsessional neurosis, the self-destructive impulses paralyze the neurotics in their daily ruminations, in hysteria, in one side, it is the life impulse and the phallic logic that drives the hysteric in their object relations. Therefore, this article seeks to 'dismantle' the hysterical symptom, building the desire in the etiology of this neurosis and showing another dynamic for its understanding.

In this book, when addressing the hysteria, I could not forget the narcissism and the body image formation. Thus, this book also brings a rereading of the neurologist Paul Schilder, providing a new vision of the body image constitution. If we start by the psychic constitution, we cannot relegate the body image constitution to a second plan. So, from a rereading of the psychoanalytic work of Sigmund Freud, Schilder presents a new vision of the body image constitution.

And, among the various manifestations of the personal order and the micro, this book brings three articles dedicated to the individual manifestations in the institutions and how these permeate the intuitional symptomatic logic. So, at this point, we will leave a micro logic and go to a meso logic that I designate as institutional.

In this logic, you, dear reader, may come across an article about the *Institutional Psychology*, specifically in the scope of the prison unit. Observing the symptomatic force field that is created in a prison unit – object of analysis in this article -, I point out that the internal relationships enable the secondary benefits from the creation and strengthening of an institutional symptom. In these mishaps, in these comings and goings, when discussing the meso level, I also bring the contributions of the book *Institutional Unconscious*, organized by Baremblitt, highlighting the contributions of the II International Symposium of Psychoanalysis (which took place in Rio de Janeiro, in 1982) for understanding the institutional symptom. And in addition to the contributions of this symposium, this book ends with the Brazilian psychiatric reform movements. Although it has taken place on Brazilian soil, the influences of the Italian Franco Basaglia contributed to the 'deinstitutionalizations' that gained a particular format in every part of this country territory. Therefore, for a better understanding of this movement, which resplends the meso level and its interfaces with the micro, we will go to the reading of these new psychoanalytic dimensions.

The Psychic Subject Constitution in the Freudian Theory

Introduction

This paper aims to address the subject psychic constitution according to the Freudian theory. For this purpose, it is necessary to go through the Viennese master early studies on the psychic constitution.

At the end of the 19th century, the time corresponding to the start of psychoanalytic theory pillars, Freud is at the beginning of his study on the psychic subject constitution. When writing the letter number twenty-four to Fliess, Freud notes:

> After periods of ten to eleven hours with the neurosis [...] I am tormented by two objectives; examine what form the mental functioning theory will assume [...] and, secondly, extract from psychopathology a profit for the normal psychology. It is impossible to have a satisfactory general conception of neuropsychotic disorders if you cannot link it to clear assumptions about the normal mental processes (1895/1996, p. 130).

So, in 1895, Freud is in the early days of the studies on the neurotic and normal processes. That same year, he focuses, on the text *Project for a Scientific Psychology*, the importance of another presence, usually the mother, at the beginning of the baby's life, for his psychic development.

According to Freud, in the psychic apparatus origin, the tension state present in the baby body, generated by the hungry tries to be released by means of a motor discharge, such as screaming and crying; but no motor discharge leads to a result for relieving his internal tension. The newborn body is incapable of a "specific action" that extinguishes the tension state, needing the help from another person. That is, of a "foreign help", from his mother (or from a substitute) through a specific action. In this way, the "satisfaction experience" puts an end to the child internal tension through the mother (or substitute) external aid to her son, having this experience the more radical implications in the development of an individual functions.

Freud resumes the satisfaction experience importance in the psychic constitution in the chapter VII of the book *The Dreams Interpretation*. In this famous book, Freud highlights that the "satisfaction experience" introduces the desire in the baby, conceiving the desire as "a psychic motion which will seek to recatechize the perception mnemonic image and retrace the own perception, that is, to re-establish the original satisfaction situation" (1900/1996, p.595). He postulates that only desire can put the psychic apparatus in motion, in accordance with the principle of pleasure. Thus, in the psychic constitution first moments, when the internal tension state created by the need arises again, the satisfactory object image is reinvested as the desire hallucinatory satisfaction.

But when publishing the text *Formulations, the Two Principles of Mental Functioning*, Freud points out:

> It will be objected that an organization that was slave of the pleasure principle and disregarded the external world reality could not keep alive, even for a shorter time [...] The use of a fiction like this, however, is justified when one considers the baby – provided that it contains the care received from the mother – almost performing a psychic system of this kind (1911/1996, p. 238).

Freud, in this quotation, is referring to the reality principle introduction in the baby psychic constitution first moments. So, after the satisfaction experience, as there is an increasing requirement of internal needs and, consequently, an absence of expected satisfaction, the child abandons this satisfaction attempt it through the hallucination. And due to the lack of satisfaction through the hallucination, a new principle of mental functioning is started: the reality principle.

After the first satisfaction experience that establishes the desire in the child, the Viennese master stresses the newborn maternal cares importance. In 1905, in the *Three Essays on Sexuality Theory*, he reiterates the importance assigned to the other, who usually is the maternal figure, in the child sexuality establishment. Thus, Freud states that:

> The child deal with the person who assists is, for him, a constant source of excitement and sexual satisfaction from erogenous zones, and even more if this person, usually the mother, admires the child with the feelings derived from her own sexual life: she touches, kisses and cradles, and it is perfectly clear that she treats him as the replacement of a fully legitimate sexual object [...] She [the mother] is awakening the her son sexual impulse and preparing its later intensity (1905/1996, p. 210-211).

The mother (or someone who replaces her), when taking care of the baby caressing and kissing him, is awakening his sexual impulse or libido. The mother (or someone who represents her) offers an endless source of sexual excitement and satisfaction of erogenous zones for her child.

And when referring to the life and death impulse presence at the child early psychic constitution, Freud postulates "that life emergence would be, then, the life continuation cause and, at the same time, of the effort towards death. And life itself would be a conflict and a conciliation between these two trends" (1923/1996, p. 53). These two trends are the two classes of impulses that coexist since birth: the life impulse (sexual impulse or libido and self-preservation impulse) and the death impulse (destructive impulse, of domain or power desire). Life consists of conflict manifestations or the interaction between these two impulsive classes, i.e., between life impulse (Eros) and death impulse (Thanatos).

These two impulse classes are present in human psyche, but Freud notes that, at the beginning, "the libido has the mission to make the destructor instinct innocuous and performs it diverting this instinct, mainly, outside [...] with the aid of a special organic system, the muscular apparatus" (1924/1996, p. 181). The death impulse deviation to the external environment is essential for the psyche constitution. The life impulse aims to make the destructive and aggressive impulse harmless, partially directing it to outside and, partially, by mixing with it.

During the first maternal cares that the individual sexual impulse arises, Freud points out:

> The child lips behave as an erogenous zone, and the stimulation by the warm milk was, no doubt, the source of pleasurable sensation [...]. Sexual activity primarily relies on one of the functions that serve for the life preservation, and only later becomes independent from them (1905/1996, p. 171).

Early in life, the baby's sexual pleasure comes from the mouth-lips excitement, the tongue. At this time, sexual activity can be related to milk intake, the lips stimulation etc.

In addition to providing that sexual pleasure, the affectionate relationship between baby and mother becomes a model for all loving relationships in the individual life. Freud declares that "the object encounter [at puberty] is, in fact, a re-encounter" (1905/1996, p. 210). This means that even after the sexual activity is separated from the nutrition act, a significant portion remains to prepare the boy to the object choice at puberty, being this object encounter a re-encounter of the old love object abandoned in remote childhood, after the Oedipus complex resolution.

From birth, the Viennese master underlines the parents' presence importance (and not only the mother) in the son psychic constitution. In relation to this presence, Freud explains:

> So they [the parents] are under the compulsion of assigning all perfections to the son [...] and hiding and forgetting all his deficiencies [...] He will once again really be the center and the creation essence – 'His Majesty the Baby' [...] The child will materialize the golden dreams that parents have never realized [...] The parents' love, so touching and in fact so childish, is nothing more than the parents' narcissism reborn, which, transformed into love object, unmistakably revels its previous nature (1914/1996, p. 97-98).

For Freud, concomitantly to the mother presence, the father is also present since the child early psychic constitution. The child birth represents for the couple (here understood as father and mother) a revival of their own narcissism that had been long abandoned. So, mom and dad relieve the old childish narcissism with their child birth, assigning all the world perfections to this new son, and denying his faults and imperfections.

According to the Freudian metapsychology, in addition to the parents' old narcissism revival with the son birth, the self-eroticism and the narcissism deserve a brief highlight in the male sex subject psychic constitution.

In a letter to Fliess, Freud already defined the self-eroticism as "a lower sexual layer [...] that acts without any psychosexual objective and only requires the local sensations of satisfaction" (1899/1996, p. 331).

Six years after writing this letter, Freud writes the *Three Essays*. In this brilliant book, which caused (and still causes) much criticism to psychoanalysis, Freud expresses that, in early life, "the impulse is not directed to another person; it is satisfied in the own body, it is the self-erotic" (1905/1996, p. 270). In other words, the baby presents a mode by which the sexual impulse finds satisfaction in his own body. And this mode is referred to as self-eroticism.

It is necessary to point out that, for Freud:

> A unit comparable to ego cannot exist in the individual since the beginning; ego must be developed. The self-erotic impulses, however, have been there since the beginning, and therefore, it is necessary that something is added to the self-eroticism – a new psychic action – to provoke the narcissism (1914/1996, p. 84).

Thus, the self-eroticism, i.e. the mode by which the impulse seeks satisfaction in the subject own body, is present since the beginning. Narcissism is the result of a new psychic action which would be added to self-eroticism.

Although not specified in the text *Regarding Narcissism: an introduction* (1914) what is this psychic action, in the article *The Instincts and its Vicissitudes*, Freud (1915) says:

> We are used to denote the ego development initial phase, during which the sexual instincts find the self-erotic satisfaction, of 'narcissism' [...]. At the very beginning of life, ego is catechized with the instincts, being, to a certain extent, able to satisfy them in ourselves. We call this condition 'narcissism' condition, and this form of obtaining satisfaction, 'self-erotic' (1915/1996, p. 137-139).

In this text, he understands narcissism as a first way in which ego is constituted, because thanks to 'his majesty, the baby' (Freud, 1914/1996, p. 84), the child's ego is organized in its early form as an ideal ego, narcissistically invested by libido and which masterpiece the boy is not willing to renounce during his childhood. Thus, the ego is a unit that does not exist since the psychic constitution beginning, needing to become, as an ideal ego, to be narcissistically invested by the parents.

It seems necessary to point out that for Freud (1923/1996), before the ideal ego resulting in narcissism, the ego is "first and foremost, a body ego; and not simply a surface entity, but it is [...] a projection of a surface" (p. 42). In the psychic early constitution, the newborn is provided of an id and, then, a body ego, targeting to the establishment of an ideal ego narcissistically invested.

On the subject psychic constitution, in addition to the ideal ego presence, it is necessary to point out the role played by pre-genital organizations.

In the libidinal development level, Freud postulates that "during the early years of a child life there are organizations in which the genital areas have hot assumed its predominant role" (1905/1996, p. 186). These organizations are defined as pre-genitals in which the impulses are partial and which objective is the satisfaction by means of the appropriate stimulation of the erogenous zone.

Freud defines the erogenous zone as "a part of the skin or mucosa where certain types of stimulation causes a pleasurable sensation of certain quality" (1905/1996, p. 187). These dominant areas are, respectively, the mouth in the oral phase and the anus in the anal phase. Still, according to Freud, "the first of these pre-genital sexual organizations is the oral, or [...] cannibalistic. In it, the sexual activity has not yet separated from nutrition, nor differentiated from the opposing currents inside it" (1905/1996, p. 186).

In this organization, sexual activity is related to the nutrition and which erogenous dominant zone is the mouth. During this organization, the child feels pleasure sucking the mother breast. That is, at the beginning of the baby's life, the psychic activity focuses on providing satisfaction to oral zones needs, such as sucking the milk from the mother breast and subsequently sucking (somehow) another object that replaces the breast, such as the finger or pacifier. The act of sucking on the mother breast is the first activity that provides pleasure to the baby, where his lips behave as an erogenous zone. Thus, sexuality begins to manifest in the baby and after breastfeeding, when he starts sucking the breast, finger or pacifier.

During the oral organization, Freud declares that the "sexual target consists in the incorporation of the object, model that later will play, in the form of identification, an important psychic role" (1905/1996, p. 187). I understand that Freud relieves in this incorporation the prototype of the first identifications of a child.

Freud returns to the identification problems in the oral organization when publishing the *Group Psychology and Ego Analysis*. In this text, Freud points out that the boy identification with his father during the phallic phase "behaves as a derivative of the first phase of libido organization, of the oral phase, in which the object that we value and for which we desire is assimilated by the ingestion in this oral or cannibalistic phase" (1921/1996, p. 115). In other words, since the oral organization the first identification of the boy with the father figure may occur. The boy may show an interest for his father, a moment in which he conceives the father figure as his ideal.

During the oral organization, Freud also recognizes that "the boy develops an object cathexis for the mother, originally related to the mother breast, and which is the prototype of an object choice according to the anaclitic model" (1923/1996, p. 44). The boy, at the same time in which he develops the identification with the father, he also develops a cathexis of sexual object regarding the mother, and the rivalry with the father is not present at this moment, which will occur only in the infant genital organization, that is, during the phallic phase.

For Freud, the second pre-genital organization is the anal-sadistic which dominant erogenous zone is the anal. In this organization, Freud says:

> The intestinal contents [...] have for the breastfeeding other important senses. It is obviously treated as a part of his own body, representing the first 'gift'. When disposing of it, the little creature can express docility to the environment surrounding him, and when refusing it, his stubbornness (1905/1996, p. 176).

During the anal-sadistic organization, the faeces represent the first gift that the child can give someone that he likes, demonstrating his obedience. If he denies giving the faeces, he is expressing his stubbornness.

Freud explains that "the fecal mass retention, at first intentionally practiced to take advantage of the stimulation as an anal zone masturbatory [...] is, by the way, one of the constipation reasons, which is so frequent in neuropaths" (1905/1996, p.176). The fecal mass retention during childhood may be related to masturbatory stimulation of anal zone, as it can also be demonstrating the pertinacity in the relationship with the people who take care of this child. And when growing, this game of retaining faeces may be symbolically present in the special scatological rituals, in ceremonial acts and similar acts which are carefully kept confidential by the neurotic individual.

Freud points out that in anal-sadistic organization "the genital zones primacy has not yet been established. On the contrary, the instinct components that dominate this pre-genital organization of sexual life are the anal-erotic and sadistic" (1913/1996, p. 345).

In a note added to *Three Essays*, Freud recognizes that, in this organization "the division into opposites that pervades the sex life has already constituted, but they still cannot be called male and female, but rather active and passive" (1915[1905]/1996, p.187). In the anal-sadistic organization, the present activity is the domination impulse through the body muscles and, as a passive sexual target organ, the intestine erogenous mucosa is found. At this infantile psychosexuality constitution phase, the primacy of the genital areas is not established yet. The antithesis between male and female does not exist, but rather the opposition between active and passive.

During this pre-genital organization, the active inclination is filled by the domain common instinct that Freud calls sadism and the passive inclination is fueled by the anal eroticism. A fortification of anal eroticism allows an inclination to homosexuality in males when the genitals primacy is achieved.

On the *New Conferences*, Freud notes that:

> The attitude towards the libido organization phases has changed a bit [...]. Whereas, previously, it was mainly emphasized the way how each phase passed before the next phase, our attention, now, is directed to the facts that show how much of each prior phase continues in the subsequent configurations [...] (1933/1996, p. 102).

Namely, the predominance of one phase in relation to the other does not occur so suddenly, but gradually, since parts of the previous organization always coexist side by side the latest.

In another footnote added to *Three Essays*, Freud revels that "after the two pre-genital organizations, there is a third phase in child development: this one, which already deserves the name of genital [...] only knows one type of genitalia: the male. For this reason, I called it the organization phallic phase" (1905/1996, p. 188). The third organization described by Freud is the infant genital organization, in which, due to the phallus primacy, is also called phallic phase. In this phase culminate the Oedipus complex and the castration complex.

The phallic phase: a brief description

For the Viennese master:

> The main characteristic of this "infant genital organization" is its difference from the adult final genital organization. It consists in the fact that, for both sexes, only one genital organ is considered, namely, the male. What is present, therefore, is not a priority of the genitals, but the phallus primacy (1923/1996, p. 158).

At this phase, both the boys and the girls only recognize one genital organ: the male. In the case of the boy, his genital organ attracts his interest; since he wants to see this part of the body in other people, to compare it with the part of his body. During his sexual researches, he comes across with the discovery that the penis is not a common possession to all people. Therefore, in the infant genital organization the phallus primacy is present, that is, the opposition of having the phallus or being castrated. This opposition is related to the Oedipus complex development and, concomitantly, the castration complex, because it is in the phallic phase that the Oedipus complex (articulated with the castration complex) reaches its apogee.

The male Oedipus complex

About the male Oedipus complex, Freud states that:

> One gets the impression that in any form the simple Oedipus complex is the [...] most common form, but it rather represents a simplification [...]. A deeper study generally revels the most complete Oedipus complex, which is duplicitous, positive and negative [...]. In my opinion, it is advisable [...] and very especially regarding the neurotic, to assume the existence of the complete Oedipus complex (1923/1996, p. 45-46).

During the infant genital organization (or phallic phase), the boy sexual desire regarding the mother acquires a greater intensity and the father figure becomes an obstacle, a rival to the realization of his incestuous desire. On the other hand, the identification with the father figure makes room for rivalry and hostility, culminating in a parricide desire, of getting rid of him with the objective of occupying his place on his mother side, thus originating the Oedipus complex. But during the infant genital organization there is not only the positive Oedipus complex development, but concomitantly to the positive complex, there is the negative Oedipus complex. This means that for Freud not only the simple positive Oedipus complex occurs in the case of the boy; but a more complete Oedipus complex, which is positive and negative, due to the bisexuality originally present in the child.

So, the boy does not present an ambivalent attitude towards his father and an object relation of unique affectionate type with his mother. This boy can also behave like a girl and show a female affectionate attitude towards the father and a corresponding jealousy and hostility towards the mother. But I highlight that it is the castration complex that puts an end to the male Oedipus complex.

The castration complex

In the text *The Infant Genital Organization*, Freud exposes that "the castration complex meaning can only be properly appreciated if its origin in the phallic primacy is also considered" (1923/1996, p. 159-160). It is in this text that it is assigned to the castration complex its fundamental place in the Freudian theory set for the infant sexuality evolution, being articulated to the Oedipus complex and the phallic phase. Therefore, the castration complex presents a close relationship with the Oedipus complex and, mainly, with the interdiction function of the boy incestuous and parricide desires towards the parents.

Freud asserts that during the infant genital organization, "the boy [...] notices the distinction between men and women, but, at first, he has no occasion to link it to a difference in his genitals" (1923/1996, p. 160). The boy assumes that all living beings and the inanimate things that surround him have a genital organ like his. This organ occupies his interest during his sexual curiosities, because he wants to see it in other people also.

During the sexual researches, when observing the genitals of his sister of little friend, the boy discovers that the penis is not present in all the people who surround him, being this lack understood as a result of castration. At this moment, the boy faces the task of reaching an agreement with castration regarding himself, since the loss of his penis becomes imaginable. Consequently, the fantasy of losing his penis gains strength every time he recalls the female genitals appearance, because the finding by the boy of the anatomical distinction of sexes is fundamental to the emergence of the castration complex.

The interlacing between Oedipus complex and the castration complex: a brief discussion on the results of the Oedipal complex dissolution.

About the Oedipus complex and its articulation with the castration complex, Freud states that:

> if the satisfaction of love in the Oedipus complex field should cost the penis to the child, it is bound to arise a conflict between his narcissistic interest in that part of his body and the libidinal cathexis of his parental objects. In this conflict, usually the first of this forces triumphs: the child ego turns its back to the Oedipus complex [...]. The Oedipus complex destruction is caused by the castration threat (1924/1996, p. 196).

In the case of the boy, the castration anxiety falls upon the complete Oedipus complex, putting an end to it. The boy, to preserve his sexual organ, gives up the pleasure he was seeking in his mother.

About the end of the Oedipus complex, Freud declares that "he sees no reason to deny the repression name to the ego's distance from the Oedipus complex, although the subsequent repressions occur mostly with the superego participation [...]" (1924/1996, p. 197). In the case of the boy, due to the castration anxiety, the ego uses the infant sexuality repression. When repressing the Oedipus complex, the boy abdicates the libidinal cathexis that was deposited on the parental figures. This cathexis is abandoned and its objects are incorporated to the ego, constituting the superego. In this way, in the closure of the male Oedipus complex, there is a repression of incestuous and parricide desires. If this fails, psychopathological manifestations may occur in the late childhood or in a later moment in the adult life of this individual.

Freud explains that:

> abandoning the Oedipus complex, a child must [...] renounce the intense object cathexis that he deposited on his parents, and it is as a compensation for this loss of objects that there is such great intensification of the identifications with his parents, which probably have been present in his ego for a long time (1933/1996, p. 69).

In the case of the boy, the object cathexis is abandoned and replaced by identifications, which were already present in his ego during the pre-genitals organizations. Therefore, with the end of the phallic phase, there is an intensification of the boy's identification with the father figure. And the identifications, having as a model the parental figures, are repeated, later, in the individual life.

At the end of the infant genital organization, Freud also expresses that "the Oedipus complex is abandoned on the boy, being repressed, destroyed, and a severe superego is installed is an heir" (1933/1996, p. 129). In the boy, in addition to a possible paternal identification (or maternal) after the repression of his Oedipus complex, the superego, and the ego ideal are the inheritors of this complex.

When referring to the ego ideal formation, Freud states:

> For the ego, the formation of an ideal would be a conditioning factor of repression [...]. What the subject projects towards himself as being his ideal [of ego] is the replacement for the narcissism lost in his childhood in which he was his own ideal [...]. The ego development consists in the removal of his primary narcissism [...]. This removal is caused by the libido displacement towards an externally imposed ego ideal (1914/1996, p. 100-102).

Thus, during the pre-genital and infant genital organization there is a narcissistic invested ideal ego. Due to the castration anxiety during the phallic phase, there is the infantile sexuality and ideal ego repression, which hers are, as stated in the previous paragraph, the superego and the ideal ego. This ideal ego is the narcissism replacement lost in childhood.

When writing *The Ego and the Id*, Freud stresses that the differentiation within the ego "can be called 'ego ideal' or 'superego'". (1923/1996, p. 43). At this time, Freud uses both concepts interchangeably, but it is only in the *New Conferences* that he elaborates a differentiation between superego and ideal ego. In these conferences, Freud declares that superego is:

> The ego ideal vehicle, by which the ego is evaluated, that stimulates it and which requirements for perfection are always greater than what he strives to accomplish [...] This ego ideal is the precipitate of the parents' old image, the admiration expression by the perfection that the child so attributed to them (1933/1996, p. 70).

I understand that Freud imputes to the superego a function of being the ego ideal vehicle responsible for the perfection pursuit, being the superego responsible for the ego ideal maintenance. Its functions are the self-observation, the consciousness and the maintenance of this ideal. On the other hand, the ego ideal has the function to stimulate the ego to achieve perfection and serve as an instrument through which ego evaluates itself.

On superego formation, Freud considers that "the father or both parents' authority is introjected in the ego, and there forms the superego core, which assumes the father severity and perpetuates his prohibition against incest, thus defeating the ego of libidinal cathexis return". (1924/1996, p. 196). Superego retains the strength, severity, and the inclination to punish that are inherited from parents. This psychic instance protects the ego against to the incestuous desires return.

For Freud:

> The child superego is, in fact, built not according to his parents' model, but his parents' superego [...] It becomes a tradition vehicle and all long-lasting value judgments that this way was transmitted from generation to generation. (1933/1996, p. 69).

Then, the superego of a boy is above all, a psychic instance where the values that go beyond his parents' superego are present, since the values and judgments are transmitted from generation to generation.

After the latency phase end (where we found the superego formation according to the Freudian conception), there begins the adult genital organization. In this organization, the "[Oedipus] complex is unconsciously revived and involved in new modifications" (Freud, 1924/1996, p. 263). At puberty, man revives in his unconscious the old Oedipal complex repressed in his early childhood. In this organization, the sexual impulses are put in the reproduction service. During puberty that one can establish a clear separation between the male and female characters, establishing the genital areas primacy that was not possible in the infant genital organization. At this phase, the man can present an object choice of anaclitic or connection object type, since it is during puberty when the adult sexual life final configuration occurs, when the object encounter is consummated, which path had been prepared from the most remote childhood.

Conclusion

Throughout this paper the core concepts linked to psychic constitution of male subject in Freudian theory were crossed, but it is necessary to highlight that due to the Oedipal complex articulation with the castration complex, each subject may present three possible exits for his infantile sexuality, i.e., three psychic destinations: neurosis, psychosis and perversion. While that, for Freud (1924), in neurosis there is the castration recognition, in psychosis occurs the refusal of it, being the delirium a bridge to the reality that was excluded. And in perversions there is a recognition, and the castration refusal, being the fetishism its prototype.

Therefore, before making a diagnosis of each clinical case, the psychotherapist is entitled to recognize his patient in the symptom singularity, listening to him in his libidinal and identification story. It is from his listening that the concepts listed above will create liveliness in the clinical practice, allowing the construction of a clinical listening.

Bibliographical Reference

FREUD, S. (1895/1996). Project for a Scientific Psychology (J. Salomão, translator). In the Brazilian Standard Edition of the complete psychological works of Sigmund Freud (vol. I, pp. 335-411). Rio de Janeiro: Imago.

FREUD, S. (1899/1996). Letter 125 (J. Salomão, translator). In the Brazilian Standard Edition of the complete psychological works of Sigmund Freud (vol. I, pp. 331-331). Rio de Janeiro: Imago.

FREUD, S. (1900/1996). The Dreams Interpretation. (J. Salomão, translator). In the Brazilian Standard Edition of the complete psychological works of Sigmund Freud (vol. V, pp. 541-655). Rio de Janeiro: Imago.

FREUD, S. (1905/1996). Three Essays on the Sexuality Theory. (J. Salomão, translator). In the Brazilian Standard Edition of the complete psychological works of Sigmund Freud (vol. VII, pp. 117-218). Rio de Janeiro: Imago.

FREUD, S. (1908/1996). Anal Character and Eroticism. (J. Salomão, translator). In the Brazilian Standard Edition of the complete psychological works of Sigmund Freud (vol. IX, pp. 159-169). Rio de Janeiro: Imago.

FREUD, S. (1911/1996). Formulations on the Two Principles of Mental Functioning. In the Brazilian Standard Edition of the complete psychological works of Sigmund Freud (vol. XII, pp. 231-243). Rio de Janeiro: Imago.

FREUD, S. (1912/1996). Contributions to a Debate on Masturbation. In the Brazilian Standard Edition of the complete psychological works of Sigmund Freud (vol. XII, pp. 257-272). Rio de Janeiro: Imago.

FREUD, S. (1913/1996). The Predisposition to Obsessional Neurosis: a contribution to the problem of the option of neurosis. (vol. XII, pp.337-349). Rio de Janeiro: Imago.

FREUD, S. (1914/1996). About Narcissism: An Introduction. In the Brazilian Standard Edition of the complete psychological works of Sigmund Freud (vol. XIV, pp. 75-110). Rio de Janeiro: Imago.

FREUD, S. (1915/1996). The Instincts and its Vicissitudes. In the Brazilian Standard Edition of the complete psychological works of Sigmund Freud (vol. XIV, pp. 115-144). Rio de Janeiro: Imago.

FREUD, S. (1915/1996). Repression. In the Brazilian Standard Edition of the complete psychological works of Sigmund Freud (vol. XIV, pp. 115-144). Rio de Janeiro: Imago.

FREUD, S. (1917/1996). XIX Conference – Resistance and Repression. In the Brazilian Standard Edition of the complete psychological works of Sigmund Freud (vol. XVI, pp. 293-308). Rio de Janeiro: Imago.

FREUD, S. (1921/1996). Group Psychology and the Ego Analysis. In the Brazilian Standard Edition of the complete psychological works of Sigmund Freud (vol. XVIII, pp. 77-154). Rio de Janeiro: Imago.

FREUD, S. (1923/1996). The Ego and the Id. In the Brazilian Standard Edition of the complete psychological works of Sigmund Freud (vol. XIX, pp. 13-80). Rio de Janeiro: Imago.

FREUD, S. (1923/1996). Infant Genital Organization: An Interpolation of Sexuality Theory. In the Brazilian Standard Edition of the complete psychological works of Sigmund Freud (vol. XIX, pp. 153-162). Rio de Janeiro: Imago.

FREUD, S. (1924/1996). Masochism Economic Problem. In the Brazilian Standard Edition of the complete psychological works of Sigmund Freud (vol. XIX, pp. 173-188). Rio de Janeiro: Imago.

FREUD, S. (1924/1996). Dissolution of Oedipus Complex. In the Brazilian Standard Edition of the complete psychological works of Sigmund Freud (vol. XIX, pp. 189-200). Rio de Janeiro: Imago.

FREUD, S. (1924/1996). Neurosis and Psychosis. In the Brazilian Standard Edition of the complete psychological works of Sigmund Freud (vol. XIX, pp. 163-172). Rio de Janeiro: Imago.

FREUD, S. (1925/ 1996). Some Psychic Consequences of Anatomical Distinction Between the Sexes. In the Brazilian Standard Edition of the complete psychological works of Sigmund Freud (vol. XIX, pp. 271-286). Rio de Janeiro: Imago.

FREUD, S. (1926/1996). Inhibitions, Symptoms and Anxiety. In the Brazilian Standard Edition of the complete psychological works of Sigmund Freud (vol. XX, pp. 79-168). Rio de Janeiro: Imago.

FREUD, S. (1933/1996). XXXI Conference – The Dissection of Psychic Personality. In the Brazilian Standard Edition of the complete psychological works of Sigmund Freud (vol. XX, pp. 63-84). Rio de Janeiro: Imago.

FREUD, S. (1933/1996). XXXII Conference – Anxiety and Instinctive Life. In the Brazilian Standard Edition of the complete psychological works of Sigmund Freud (vol. XX, pp. 85-112). Rio de Janeiro: Imago.

FREUD, S. (1940/1996). Psychoanalysis Outline. In the Brazilian Standard Edition of the complete psychological works of Sigmund Freud (vol. XXIII, pp. 151-208). Rio de Janeiro: Imago.

MASSON, J. M. (1986). The complete correspondence of Sigmund Freud to Wilhelm Fliess 1887-1904. Rio de Janeiro: Imago.

Contributions from Piera Aulagnier to Freudian metapsychology: an approach on the originary, primary and secondary functioning modes for the 'I' constitution.

Introduction

The French psychoanalyst Piera Aulagnier, at the end of the 60s, along with other Lacanian dissident psychoanalysts, founded the Quatrième Groupe, a group that would not be connected to the Lacanian orthodoxy. Aulagnier never denied the importance and influence of Lacan in her way of thinking the psychoanalysis, but she "leaves absolutely clear that she is Freudian – as the French psychoanalysts who followed Lacan only until the first phase of his productions are considered, when he proposed to return to Freud" (2001, p. 10). Due to the richness and uniqueness of her clinic, certain clinic questions of the Freudian legacy were emerging during her vast experience with psychotics' parents.

These questions can be replied by this famous phrase of Aulagnier:

> Confronted to psychosis, we find out that Freud model did not respond to some of these questions and [...] we have seen that the application of this model to the response that the discourse raised in us, kept excluded a part of our own experience [...]. It was necessary to recognize that, from the moment that we privileged a particular form of questioning, the model showed anomalies, whatever was the psyche functioning to which it was applied (1975/1979, p. 17).

Therefore, based on her clinic with psychotic patients, Aulagnier came across the boundaries that the Freudian model presented to treat this form of psychic suffering and its analyzability; since for Freud, the psychotic does not make the transfer and, therefore, could not benefit from an analysis. It is necessary to emphasize that the Freudian clinic was based on the analysis of adult neurotic patients. And by enabling the psychotics analysis, Aulagnier presents metapsychological, psychopathological, methodological, technical and ethical contributions to the Freudian legacy, thus responding to the Freudian pointing that only with future developments in psychoanalysis, this could become accessible to the psychotics' analysis.

According to Aulagnier "every individual is born in a 'speaking space' and that is why, before we discuss the 'I' structure as an instance constituted by the speech, we will analyze the conditions necessary to ensure that this space offers the 'I' a habitat suitable to its demands" (1975/1979, p. 105). For the advent of the 'I', not only the maternal desire is important for the psychic constitution of the future child, but also the fatherly desire regarding this child; since the child is born in a family space organized by the speech and by the desire of the parental couple between themselves and regarding that baby.

On the other hand, what would that 'I' be to Aulagnier? First, it is necessary to point out that the 'I' belonging to the metapsychology of Aulagnier is different from the Freudian ego. For Freud "[...] a unit comparable to ego cannot exist in the individual since the beginning; ego must be developed" (1914/1996, p. 84). Freud does not specify the date on which this ego is constituted, being the narcissism the first form in which the ego is constituted as ideal ego; since the parents, when reliving their own narcissism during their child birth, they raise this to the level of their 'majesty, the baby'. And the master still stresses that "ego is, first and foremost, a bodily ego"

(1923/1996, p. 39). This ego is the result of bodily sensations, especially those arising from the body surface.

Regarding the Freudian ego, Aulagnier says:

> For me, 'I' is an instance that is directly linked to language. There is no place in my metapsychological conception to the undifferentiated ego-id concept. In this sense, one cannot make an equivalence between the manner how Freud uses the ego concept [...] and what I have defined as 'I'. I defined a fundamental concept for me that is the anticipated 'I' and we cannot talk about an anticipated ego in the maternal speech [...] (2010, p. 63).

For Aulagnier, this 'I' is a historical 'I' that inserts the baby, since its birth, in a temporal and symbolic order; since this 'I' is born immersed in the parents' Oedipal story and is constituted through identificatory dialectic. About this, she points out that "my difference with Lacan is that, for me, the 'I' is not condemned to ignorance, nor it is a passive instance. Although their first identified are provided by maternal speech, the 'I' is also an identifying instance and it is not a passive product of the Other speech" (2010, p. 63). As this 'I' is anticipated by the maternal desire, this 'I' cannot be considered the equivalent to the Lacanian 'I', because this instance consists of two dimensions: the identified (provided by the maternal speech) and the identifying (which is not the passive product of the Other). On the other hand, this 'I' is also structured by language to the extent that, even before coming into the world, the infants[1] are pre-enunciated and pre-invested by the parental couple speech. This baby is born in a family entourage, a "micro-environment", which Aulagnier defines as the "speaking space" (1975/1979, p. 105).

---

1   According to Pierre Kaufmann, infans is "a term which the own Lacan uses to qualify the child before he uses the language [...]". In: *Encyclopedic Dictionary of Psychoanalysis: the legacy of Freud to Lacan*. Rio de Janeiro, Jorge Zahar, 1998, p.157.

Therefore, this future 'I' will develop in a family micro-environment organized by the parents' speech, by the desire that unites
the parents and by the desire of each of them for this child.

For Aulagnier:

> Preceding the individual birth pre-exists a speech regarding
> him: a kind of spoken shadow and alleged by the mother that
> speaks, she just over the infants' body – at his birth – taking
> the place of this to whom the spokesman's speed is addressed to
> [...]. The mother [...] imputes to the shadow a desire that she is
> unaware [...]. What we call shadow is, therefore, constituted of a
> series of enunciations that witness the maternal desire regarding
> the child; they constitute an identificatory image that anticipates
> what will be enunciated by the voice of this body, still absent
> (1975/1979, p. 109-113).

In other words, this shadow is the heiress of the mother
Oedipal story; as well as of her repressed. This shadow anticipates the child own repressed, allowing a reorganization of the
future baby psychic space; since the mother transmits the baby a
repressed necessary for the structuring of its future 'I', being this
repressed the predecessor of the role played by a third reference,
that is the father. In addition, this shadow safeguards the return
of her repressed desire of having a child of her own father. So,
the mother performs the function of the spokesperson, inserting
the baby in the environment speech, point out him the laws and
requirements of it.

In 1979, when publishing *The Destinies of Pleasure*, this
psychoanalyst resumes the 'I' constitution, highlighting that
"for the I life being possible, it is necessary that the spokesperson
has invested the 'I' that it anticipates, providing him thoughts
with identificatory function, while the 'I' cannot think them or
invent them" (1979/1985, p. 139). The baby image built along
the pregnancy, the quality and intensity of this investment are
fundamental for his future psychical development. The baby 'I',

as previously mentioned, is anticipated by the mother 'I'; once that since birth, the mother interprets, in terms of feelings, the pictographic activities manifestations of the baby psychic apparatus. On the first encounters between the baby real body and the psychic representation that the mother elaborates about it, these encounters can be a source of (dis) pleasure for the newborn. This means that the mother anticipates a body still absent, libidinally formulating pre-enunciations and pre-investment of this body, thus constituting a 'spoken body' that, in turn, is expected to anchor in the baby actual body.

On the other hand, it is necessary to emphasize that to Aulagnier the 'I' is constituted between the 6th and the 18thmonthes (during the Lacanian mirror stage); but before this 'I' coming by means of the speculate or imagined identification, the other psychic functioning modes will represent the lived in the baby psyche: these are the originary, the primary and the secondary (which correspond to the 'I' advent).

To address these three psychic functioning modes, it is necessary to point out what would be the representation activity. For Aulagnier:

> By representation activity we understand the psychic equivalent of metabolizing work characteristic of the organic activity [...] The absorbed and metabolized element [by psyche] is not a physical body, but a transformation element. If we consider the representation activity as a common task to psychic processes, it can be said that its purpose is to metabolize an element of heterogeneous nature into a homogeneous element to the structure of each system (1975/1979, p. 27).

For Aulagnier it is this representation activity that oversees registering in the existing psyche, the lived, and all information to be represented; this must be invested of libido. The psychic activity is constituted by the set, as Aulagnier says, "of three functioning modes, or by three metabolizing processes"

(1975/1979, p. 28). These three-psyche metabolizing or functioning processes are the originary process, the primary process and the secondary process, which representations are, respectively, the pictographic representation or pictogram, the phantasmal representation, and the ideating representation (in the secondary process).

Regarding the psychic functioning modes, Aulagnier postulates that the originary, primary and secondary processes "are not immediately present in the psychic activity: they occur temporarily and the emergence of each of them results from the need that is imposed to the psyche for becoming aware of an object property, outside it, a property that the previous process had the obligation to ignore [...]"(1975/1979, p. 28).These three psychic functioning modes that produce the representation of the lived are not present in activities since birth. Although Aulagnier has not established dates, we can point out that the originary is in activity since birth, being succeeded by the primary entrance and, at the time of the 'I' advent, by the secondary. This is how all lived will be metabolized by these three processes that will coexist in a more or less conflictive manner.

The Originary Process

Aulagnier declares that "the originary encounter, in principle, occurs at the time of birth [...]. When we talk about originary time, it is to this starting point that we refer" (1975/1979, p. 41). During the birth, at the time of the inaugural encounter mouth-breast, it comes onto scene the originary functioning mode, a mode that is prior to the primary process. The originary process activity requires the encounter between a sensorial organ (such as the mouth) and an external object (like the breast) that comes to stimulate it. This is a process that precedes the entry onto the scene of the Freudian primary process and which encounter in the baby psyche is registered through a pictographic representation or pictogram.

For Aulagnier "the pictographic representation of this encounter has the particularity of ignoring the duality that composes it [...]. We say since now that the essential conduction is that this experience may be represented as causing pleasure to the both entities that we will define as 'object-complementary zone'" (1975/1979, p. 43-44). Due to the requirement of representability, the representation activity of this functioning mode registers in the baby psyche an 'image of body thing'; that is, an image of zone-object-complement. On the other hand, according to this psychoanalyst, the pictographic representation, that is pulsional, does not recognize the mouth separated from the breast; in other words, the sensory organ represented by the erogenous zone (mouth) and the external complementary object (breast) are pictographically represented as a unit that can be connected (if the experience is pleasurable), becoming fusional; or they repel it, if there is a displeasure. Thus, the only psychic registration mode of this functioning mode is sensorial, providing pleasure or displeasure to the baby.

It should be reminded that at birth, the baby's incipient psyche finds two fragments of the world: his own body and the others psyche, starting with the maternal 'I'. This first encounter with the mother is essential for the beginning of the baby psychic constitution; because in addition to the vital need of food, there is an entire libidinal investment of the mother towards her son, an investment that is essential for the psychic functioning. This experience should provide at least a minimum of pleasure and will be psychically represented by the originary. Therefore, this psychoanalyst understands the satisfaction experience as the occasion of the inaugural encounter mouth-breast. It is at this encounter that coincides, just once, the maternal desire that the newborn demands her breast, and the baby demand that the mother desires him, from what results in the baby primary identification with the coextensive perceptions to the maternal response to his primary demand.

About this emergence of the 'I' in the psychic scenario, Aulagnier points out that "for founding his history, [this I] will have to find a way and a voice that make it possible to think this before" (1984/1989, p. 215). In the primary identification, the baby comes across a body external to him and which presence is an immediate relief of his libidinal demand. And to 'think this before', this I must be pre-invested by his mother. On the other hand, this is "before it can be alternately revealed as an ally or an adversary" (1984/1989, p. 216). This ally can be a source of pleasure and investment for the baby; or, on the contrary, the presence of this opponent can become a source of displeasure, and not of libidinal investment by the baby.

At birth, "the breast opens the game and it will have, in the primary identification, a determinative function" (1984/1989, p. 201). If for the mother the breast is identified as the object that the baby demands as the target of his desire, this demand becomes for the mother a source of love, of life, symbolizing the maternal function and becoming her most precious emblem. In other words, it will always be by the breast offer that the mother will respond the demand of her baby; since the breast offers the first support for the libidinal demand, exerting the function of the first significant of the maternal desire, playing a dual role during the primary identification: the breast becomes the mold, the matrix, of this identification both for the maternal significant and for the pre-specular identification. So, at this moment, there is a fusion of the two desires which present a significant in common: the breast as an object of demand for the baby and of maternal offer, this occurring with a double alienation of the baby in the desire and in the maternal imaginary[2].

2　The double alienation (of the baby in the desire and in the maternal imaginary) is notorious in cases of psychosis in adulthood.

The Primary Process

The originary process works alone just for some moments. To account for the maternal absence and return that occurs due to the separation between the baby body and the maternal body, the primary functioning mode appears. This mode represents the lived in the psyche through a fantasy. So, as the originary process does not recognize any sign of relation, the primary begins to function since very early to account for the alternation of the maternal presence and absence; as well as the pleasure and displeasure arising from this presence or absence.

In this mode of functioning, what characterizes its production mode "is a figuration in which, effectively, there is a representation of two spaces; but these two spaces are subjected to the omnipotence of a single desire [...]" (1975/1979, p. 70). The imputation of the lived caused to the omnipotence of the Other desire (in other words, the desire of the own baby projected in one of the parents or in both) is the principle that governs the primary. All pleasure or displeasure lived in consecutive encounters with the 'I' of the Other and with the external reality are represented in the psyche and attributed to the Other desire to give or refuse pleasure; since this Other[3] functions as a support that every child needs to be constituted of. Thus, the displeasure caused by the separation and the pleasure of the encounter, which satisfies the baby needs and pacifies his pulsional motions, can only be the purpose of the Other desire, and the union and separation acts, assigned by the baby as a manifestation, respectively, of love or hate.

It is in the primary that the primary scene is psychically registered, composing the core of every phantasmal organization

---

3 This Other can be the mother of the father that allude a cultural order for the baby.

present in the pictographic engram[4]; that is, of appropriating or rejecting. Even before any possible understanding of the coitus between the patents, there is a model of functioning that is supported in the model of an 'act' that aims the union of a part of one body to another body, penetrating it, being in this case, an 'act' of love; or an act that aims to keep off the part which he desires the destruction, being this an 'act' of hatred.

I believe that at this point it is necessary to answer a question that I consider to be central in this paper: when occurs the father's entry onto the scene? On the entry of the 'other without breast' onto the scene, Aulagnier says:

> Our assertion that the entry in the primary function implies in the recognition of the presence of a breast separated from the own body, made us put aside what follows it: the recognition of the 'other-without-breast', invested by the first representative of the Other in the real scene, through which the father existence and the recognition of the parental couple are preannounced to the psyche (1975/1979, p. 74).

From this other space that is occupied by the attributes that testify the paternal presence, this space points to the existence of an enigmatic object that enables the Other to accomplish a desire that no longer refers to that one who contemplates the scene that, in this case, would be the child. Consequently, from the entrance of the father onto the scene, "the infrastructure of the three elements will be organized, which is the structure of the whole phantasmal organization" (1975/1979, p. 74). This organization is formed by the representative of the Other (such as the mother), by the other space (which is occupied by the father's entry onto the scene) and by the look (of the baby)

---

4   According to Violante, "the pictographic engram is a mnesic trait not assimilable to an image". VIOLANTE, Maria Lucia V. *PieraAulagnier: a contribution to the Work of Freud*. São Paulo: via Leterra, 2001, p. 35.

that realizes an affection of pleasure assigned to the relationship existing between the parents.

For Aulagnier "since the first phase of its activity, the primary establishes the prototypes of the secondary, without which the psyche could not have access to what will become the third representation of its relation to the world" (1975/1979, p. 74). These prototypes or models allude to the reality, to the 'I', to castration and the Oedipus complex (which primary scene is its prototype in this psychic functioning mode). So, with the beginning of the primary functioning, these four secondary prototypical functioning modes are introduced into the baby psyche.

The first prototype is related to reality. In this prototype, Aulagnier ensures that the "reality of the Other is, for us, the reality of the difference present between the mother desire and the infants desire" (1975/1979, p. 75). In case the difference between the mother and the baby desire disappears or becomes a too small difference, this will disable the pulsional game, running the risk of disappearing from the phantasmal scene, which Aulagnier points as the 'third pole'; that is, the look.

And regarding the second prototype, the identificatory prototype, Aulagnier points out that this "as a precursor of the 'I', assigning the representation of the 'imaginative' that is the result of the reflection of the primary activity on itself, a reflection that is the source of what we call the unconscious individual" (1975/1979, p. 76). In other words, what precedes the 'I' in the primary process is the subject of the unconscious. This precursor is formed as an image of the response given to the desire projected on the mother; as well as the introjection of a sign considered as an evidence of the Other presence to give or refuse pleasure. Thus, through a pulsional dialectic between projection and introjection, the unconscious individual identifies with the response to the maternal desire.

Regarding the Oedipus prototype, Aulagnier ensures that to this 'scenic figuration the 'Oedipal' quality of what is going on in the outside scene is added [...]" (1975/1979, p. 79). It should be remembered that the primary scene is the prototype of the Oedipus complex in the primary. This means that, in the primary, the precedent of the Oedipus complex is formed by the remnants of the parental Oedipus. If on one side this child is the historicized successor of the child that one day each of the parents wished to have; on the other, as a phantasmal representation of the primary scene is constituted by three elements, in the outside scene the baby psyche observes the emergence of the 'other-without-breast'.

This emergence may be a source of pleasure for the set of the erogenous zone-functions, making the presence of this father desired by the baby; or, on the contrary, this presence may become disruptive and displeasurable to the baby. That is how every fantasy has in itself a scene with three elements: the look of the baby contemplating a scenario in which there are two objects (desired or not) present.

But how does the entrance of the desire of this 'another without breast' occur? For Aulagnier "from the moment when the child puts the mother desire as different from his, she should figure another object, which is not her own, for this desire" (1975/1979, p. 78). This means that when the child realizes the possibility of a desire of the Other for 'another space', removing her from her exclusive space of pleasure, the child necessarily renounces this joyous space which he believed to be the exclusive object of the mother and that the mother desired as the unique object of his pleasure.

In her interview to Hornstein, Aulagnier discusses about the entrance of the father onto the scene, saying that:

> since the beginning of the life the father exercises a modifier action on the environment which surrounds the newborn. But, in almost all cases, a person – usually the mother – has a key role in

New Psychoanalytic Dimensions

the response to the baby's needs – both the 'I'-conservation and the libidinal ones. That is why from her will appear the first sign of the father presence or of his absence, and the choice of these signs will depend on her relation with this father" (2010, p. 58).

This father, from the cries and screams of his baby, can offer him a body pleasure, caressing him, relieving him of displeasure through his touches and words and, as Aulagnier points out, "making resonate in his ears the phonemics sequence, which tone transforms it into a lullaby, which the maternal voice is no longer the only emitter" (1975/1979, p. 79). This means that from the moment that the presence of this 'other-without-breast' is recognized by the child, this presence can become a source of body pleasure for him, revealing to the set of his erogenous zones-functions as a source of pleasure, even if that presence can, at certain times, become disturbing.

And before going to the secondary process, it is necessary to point out the last prototype present in the primary functioning mode: this last prototype would be the castration.

Regarding this prototype, Aulagnier points out:

> [...] every event, in the world, will be identified, by the one who looks, an accident in his own body or the body of the Other, since the affection experienced by the psyche can only be represented by the erogenous zones images, of the maternal body or, the own body, that is, by a relation that unites the representatives of the body space. No matter that this is the maternal body or his own [body], since the contemplation of the aggression of the maternal body or, conversely, its plenitude, puts that one that looks in a position of mutilated or unified, a consequence of the desire attributed to the scenario actors (1975/1979, p. 81).

In the primary activity, the baby psyche cannot capture an external event without representing it as the cause of his desire, seeking the pleasure of his own body space. Every pleasure experience has an integrating effect due to the pleasure experienced. On the other hand, every displeasure activity supposes to be mutilating; because, in this case, the function zone and the object figure what the baby's look finds add a rejecting-rejected, presupposing the fantasy of being mutilated. So, in this psychic functioning mode, the mutilation anguish becomes a precursor of the castration anguish.

Regarding the amputation anguish, Aulagnier continues by stating that "the primary is able to [...] connect scenic fragments and the succeeding scenes [...]. The importance of mutilation as a castration prototype confirms that the primary is, effectively, the creator of prototypes and that the secondary inherits and transforms it, without ever being sure that they cannot return to their first form" (1975/1979, p. 83). Aulagnier points out that the productions resulting from these functioning modes comprise two non-homogeneous sets. The first set corresponds to the scenic primary and it is exemplified by the image of the thing. And in a second moment of the primary, there is the entrance onto the scene of the word image and that, when uniting to the thing image, it allows the entrance onto the scene of the mixed productions; in other words, the meaning system imposed by the speech.

In this second moment "the characteristic [...] is to possess the quality of the speakable and, therefore, the quality of the conscious" (1975/1979, p. 84). On the primary already occurs the participation of the principle of reality. If at the first time of this functioning mode the primary produces the thing image, on the second moment, this thing image comes to add the word image as a primary meaning and not as a linguistic sign. The word image is formed by the phonetic sequence heard by the baby, informing the primary about the intention of the maternal desire of giving or refusing pleasure, respectively. Thus, the image of thing represents a transition element; since this image comes shortly after the pictographic activity and, at the same time, precedes the speakable, a moment in which the thing representation is connected to a word representation.

For Aulagnier, in the primary, "the libidinal sense transcends the linguistic meaning, but it opens the way for it, inducing the psyche to admit that this meaning exists: that it is part of the spokesperson heritage and that it is related to the offer or refusal present in his response" (1975/1979, p. 97). It is the libidinal sense of the first primary meanings that paves the way for the linguistic meanings that will only be accepted by the 'I' of the baby with the arrival of the enunciations pronounced by the father, the first representative of the others. This representative points out that all and any enunciation is governed by a linguistic code shared by the sociocultural environment, regardless of the others desire. Therefore, the primary meanings open path to the ideating activity present in the secondary mode of functioning. This activity is the result of the 'I', an instance that recognizes the linguistic sign and the interpretative system characteristic of this functioning mode.

Secondary Process

And for approaching the secondary, it is necessary to emphasize that for Aulagnier "the three processes [originary, primary and secondary] are not immediately present in the psychic activity; they temporarily occur [...]" (1975/1979, p. 28). The entrance onto the scene of the secondary functioning coincides with the advent of the 'I'. Therefore, the secondary is the psychic functioning mode that is characteristic of the 'I' or enunciating instance.

Regarding the secondary, Aulagnier declares that:

> from the given moment, which marks the passage of the infants' state to the child, the psyche will jointly acquire the first rudiments of language and a new 'function' will result from the constitution of a third psychic place, in which all existing shall acquire the status of 'thinkable', necessary for it acquiring the

sayable attribute. This sayable thought can be defined by the term of intelligible: so, a 'intellection function' is established, which product will be the ideating flow that will accompany the activity set, from the most elementary to the most elaborate, of which the 'I' can be the agent (1975/1979, p. 59).

Aulagnier understands the passage from the baby state to the child from the moment of the beginning of the functioning of the secondary functioning mode, through which occurs the acquisition of the first rudiments of the language. In the secondary, all the 'I' activity is translated into a thinking flow; this means that the speakable, the intelligible becomes the attribute of the 'I' productions. Thus, every experience will only exist if it can be followed by an idea that makes it thinkable and speakable.

Such idea is reiterated in *The Destinies of Pleasure*, when she points out that "what characterizes the 'I' is to represent and self-represent the existing [...] in the form of a construction of ideas. To do so, one should be able to add to the thing image, the word image and invest in the last one" (1979/1985, p. 19). The products resulting from this functioning mode are the ideas (ideating representations) and the enunciations. In this psychic functioning mode, the 'I' attributes everything that is lived to an intelligible causality. This is the postulate that governs the enunciating instance.

When the secondary mode of the psychic functioning begins to work, the erogenous zones unify, providing the foundation for the emergence of the demand vehicle of the subject: the language. For Aulagnier "the first role that the subject makes the language perform is exactly that to transmit his demand" (1968/1990, p. 194). It is on and by the demand that the subject constitutes his language in speech; since at the moment in which the subject ego speaks, this ego demands to the Other, to himself and his alike the satisfaction of his pre-genital demands. So, as the baby gets acquainted with the language handling, he uses it to demand his objects with phallic glow.

When discussing the 'I' constitution during the secondary process and its respective peculiarities, Aulagnier also points out that:

> the particularity of the 'I' lies in the fact that, at the beginning, it was effectively the idea, the name, the thought spoken by the speech of another: spoken shadow, projected by the spokesperson [...] The 'I' starts investing in the 'identifying thoughts' by which the spokesperson thinks it, and thanks to which he transmits his love [...]" (1979/1985, p. 21).

The spokesperson, through his desire and his speech, presents an identificatory function, but it is also responsible for presenting the child a reality remodeled by his own psyche. Remember that the 'I' is anticipated, historicized and structured by the language; and by the desire and the parental couple speech (which present an identificatory function) and by the speech of the entourage. Therefore, this anticipated 'I' is understood as the moment in which the child is inserted into a temporal and symbolic order.

In 1979, when writing *Necessary Pleasure and Sufficient Pleasure*, Aulagnier emphasizes that, for the 'I' existence, the human reality in which the subject is inserted shall allow the functioning preservation of his body and his psychic activity of representing pictographic, phantasmal and ideationally as a condition necessary for this 'I' investing in the reality, in himself and in his body; but also in the others and in reality. On the other hand, it is necessary to emphasize that the 'I' is constituted by means of an identificatory dialectic in which path Aulagnier highlights in the foreground two fundamental moments: the moment of the 'I' advent (during the speculate identification) and that of the 'I' assuming the symbolic castration (during the symbolic identification).

Regarding the speculating or imaginative identification, Aulagnier points out that "this is [...] the second time of the identificatory dialectic" (1968/1990, p. 201). After the primary identification – an identification precursor of the 'I', in which moment the mother desires that the infants demand, and the infants demand that the mother desires – Aulagnier highlights a second moment of the identificatory dialectic: the speculate identification. In this second moment occurs the advent of the 'I' in which it identifies with the response to the maternal desire. So, for Aulagnier, the 'I' is not present since the beginning of the psychic constitution, and it might be constituted between the 6th and the 18th months, at the phase of the mirror that Lacan discusses.

This first mode in which the 'I' is constituted alone is possible due to the satisfactions of the pre-genital demands of the child; namely, the satisfaction of his object demands. These demands may be considered phallic equivalents (such as the breast, faeces, penis) and which, when being encoded as a maternal gift, support the child desire. Therefore, the object demands are pre-genital demands of the child addressed to the Other (such as to the mother) and these prevent the child alienation in the field of the Other, providing, on one hand, the joyous assumption of himself and, on the other, the differentiation of the maternal 'I', causing the aggression involved in this process.

And the third moment of this identificatory dialectic would be the symbolic identification. This comprises two times: the "time to understand", which is extended from the advent of the 'I' in the phase of the mirror until the castration assumption, and the "time to conclude", which begins with the castration and culminates with the identification to the identificatory project (a project that corresponds to the Freudian ego ideal).

But how does the relation of the parental couple desire occur regarding this son at this moment of the 'I' constitution? This psychoanalyst stresses that the child "confronted with the reality of the father desire and of the mother for the latter, it is the incest prohibition that he finds there, where he expected to find the desire achievement" (1968/1990, p. 214). If this child does not renounce the demand destined to his mother, this may be undervalued and cut from his family field where he would find the identificatory references coextensive to his possibility of putting himself as the subject. On the other hand, if this child desired to know the truth about the mother desire object, what she has in response to this desire, her demand, is the 'father name'. And when recognizing the father presence, this figure comes to introduce the instance of law, interdicting this mother. So, it is the name of the father the unique that has the power of offering the language statute of the subjects, being the father the owner of the keys that will give access to his symbolic world.

Conclusion

From the three psychic functioning modes, it can be stated that both the maternal and the paternal desires are present since the baby birth. The understanding of the uniqueness and intensity of these desires are necessary for the libidinal and identificatory history analysis of each individual.

As the baby 'I' is pre-enunciated and pre-invested by the mother, it should not be forgotten that the baby image built along the pregnancy, the quality and intensity of this investment are fundamental for his future psychical development. On the other hand, this 'I' is born immersed in the parents' Oedipal story, constituting in his own Oedipal story through an identificatory dialectic.

For understanding this identificatory dialectic and how this 'I' is based, this paper reviewed the three psychic functioning modes: the originary, the primary and the secondary. Remembering that, at the time of birth, the only psychic functioning mode is the originary. This is the most primitive, archaic, psychic functioning mode, which lasts a few moments, being followed by the primary mode; since the reality of the absence and return of the mother requires its entrance. In this, we have two spaces (the mother and the baby) under the omnipotence of the desire of only one. And when acquiring the first rudiments of language, the baby psyche will conquer a new function in which all lived will acquire the status of thinkable, speakable, intelligible, which ideating flow will follow the set of activities, from the most elementary to the most elaborate, among which only the 'I' can be its agent.

When a more elaborate mode of psychic functioning, such as the secondary, cannot provide sense to the lived in order to register is psychically by means of an ideating representation, the most primitive psychic functioning modes will do it, such as the primary and/or the originary. Therefore, an analysis of these three psychic functioning modes is essential for understanding the 'I' constitution and how these experiences are psychically registered.

Bibliographical Reference

AULAGNIER, P. (1968/1990). *An interpreter in the Search of Meaning* – I. São Paulo: Escuta.

AULAGNIER, P. (1975/1979). *The Violence of Interpretation – from pictogram to the enunciated.* Rio de Janeiro: Imago.

AULAGNIER, P. (1979/1985). Necessary Pleasure and Sufficient Pleasure. In: *The Destinies of Pleasure.* Rio de Janeiro: Imago.

AULAGNIER, P. (1984/1989). *The Historian Apprentice and the Wizard Master.* São Paulo: Escuta.

FREUD, S. (1914/1996). About the Narcissism: An Introduction. *ESB*, vol. XIV. Rio de Janeiro: Imago.

FREUD, S. (1923/1996). The Ego and the Id. *ESB,* vol. XIX. Rio de Janeiro: Imago.

HORNSTEIN, L. (2010). Dialogue with Piera Aulagnier. In: *Desire and identification*. Org. Maria Lucia Vieira Violante. São Paulo: Annablume.

KAUFMANN, P. (1998).*Encyclopedic Dictionary of Psychoanalysis: the legacy of Freud to Lacan.*Rio de Janeiro, Jorge Zahar.

VIOLANTE, M. L. V. (2001). *PieraAulagnier: A Contemporary Contribution to the Work of Freud.*São Paulo: Via Leterra Editora.

VIOLANTE, M. L. V. (2010). *Desire and Identification.* São Paulo: Annablume.

The obsessional thought in the conception of Sigmund Freud

The obsessional thought

This paper aims to develop a review on the psychoanalytic work of Sigmund Freud about the thought in obsessional neurosis, pointing out its main characteristics. For this development, it will be necessary to make a brief return to the early writings of Freud on this neurosis.

In 1894, in letter 18 to Fliess, Freud points out that there is an affection displacement in the obsession, and this statement is reiterated in the article *The Neuropsychosis of Defense* of 1894, when he says:

> "When someone with a predisposition to neurosis lacks ability for the conversion […] this affection is obliged to remain on the psychic sphere. The representation, now weakened, persists in the consciousness, separated from any association. But his affection, made free, connects to other representations which are not incompatible in themselves, and thanks to this false connection, such representations become obsessional representations" (1894, p. 58 – 59).

At this time, Freud was in the primordium of his studies on the obsessional ideas formation, stating that not all who suffer from obsessions have such a clear idea about its origin.

Freud (1894, p. 59) understands that "[...] the obsession represents a substitute for the incompatible sexual idea taking its place in the consciousness". He stresses that the affection present in the obsessions is characterized as displaced or transposed and this can be, in many cases of obsessions, retranslated in sexual terms. The self takes much less advantage choosing by the affection transposition as a defense methodology and the affection remains like before, unchanged and not diminished, differing "only in the fact that the incompatible representation is muffed and insulated from memory" (1894, p. 61). Thus, Freud understands that the defense aims to separate the incompatible representation of affection; in other words, the idea would remain in the consciousness (weakened and isolated), but isolated from the affection.

According to Freud (1895, p. 82), "in the obsessions, the emotional state persists indefinitely and the associated idea is no longer the original appropriate idea related to the obsession etiology, but an idea that displaces it, being a replacement for it". At this time, Freud also understands that in obsessional ideas, the original representation (incompatible) was replaced by another representation and the original idea may not be replaced by another idea, but by acts or impulses that would originally serve as relief measures or as protective procedures.

The obsessional idea, according to Freud, is the product of a commitment: correct regarding the affection and the present category, however it would be false due to the chronological displacement and the replacement by analogy. For the master (1896 a, p. 271) "the self-censorship affection can be transformed, by different psychic processes, which later enter the conscience more clearly than the affection itself". This affection can be transformed into anxiety, delusions of persecution, shame, anguish and the conscious ego can consider obsession as something that is strange to it. He claims that in the obsessional neurosis occurs a defensive struggle of the ego against the obsession, leading to the production of new secondary defensive symptoms. The obsessional idea is attacked by the logic, although its compulsive strength is unshakeable. The secondary symptoms are an intensification of scrupulosity and a compulsion to thoroughly peer things and keep them.

According to Freud (1896 a, p. 272), "other secondary symptoms arise if the compulsion is transferred to motor impulses against the obsession, for example, the compulsion for drinking, protective rituals, folie du doute". The ego seeks to keep off the derivate of the memory initially repressed and in this defensive struggle creates symptoms that could be classified as secondary defense.

For Freud (1896 b, p. 173) "the secondary defense against the obsessional representations can be performed by a violent deviation to other thoughts of content as opposed as possible. That is why the obsessional rumination, when successful, regularly deals with abstract and supra-sensual things". The secondary defense against the obsessional affections would lead to a set of protective measures capable of being transformed into obsessional acts, such as penitential measures (numbers observation), precautionary measures (such as superstition, thoroughness).

The obsessional thought in psychoanalytic texts (1900- 1939)

Due to his self-analysis, Freud abandons the traumatic theory of neurosis in 1897, resuming the study on obsessional thought in 1907, in *Obsessive Acts and Religious Practices*. In this article, the master highlights that "people who engage in obsessional or ceremonial acts belong to the same class of those that suffer of obsessional thought, obsessional ideas, obsessional impulses, and related. This, together, constitutes a special clinical entity that is commonly called obsessional neurosis" (1907, p. 109). Therefore, in the clinical entity called obsessional neurosis, we find people who practice ceremonial (or obsessional) acts but also people who exhibit obsessional impulses and obsessional ideas, and not all ideas or impulses end in ceremonial acts.

In this same text, Freud points out that in the obsessional thought there are two defense mechanisms: the displacement and the reactive formation. Regarding the displacement mechanism, the master states that the mechanisms of psychic displacement dominate the mental processes of obsessional neurosis; since the symbolism of the obsessional act is the result of the replacement of a real and important element by a trivial one.

And regarding the reactive formation, he claims that there is always the repression of an instinctive impulse that succumbed to repression. In other words, it is due to the repression that a special consciousness is created, directed against the instinct objectives; because the repression in this neurosis "is a process that only obtains partial success; being constantly under the threat of failure [...] Thus, the ceremonial and obsessional acts arise, in part, as a protection against a temptation, in part, as a protection against the expected evil" (1907, p. 114 – 115).

In addition to the repression failure, Freud associates the anal character with the thought of the neurotic. For Freud:

> "In reality, wherever they have prevailed or even persist in archaic forms of thought – in ancient civilizations, in myths, fairy tales and superstitions, in unconscious thought, in dreams and neurosis - the money is closely related to dirt [...] the original erotic interest in defecation is destined to become extinct in later years. On this occasion appears the interest for the money, which did not exist in childhood" (1908, p. 162 -163).

In obsessional thought one can find the traits resulting from the anal eroticism sublimation; such as the order, parsimony and obstinacy. These traits will be resumed in the text *The Transformations of Instinct Exemplified in anal Eroticism*, in 1917, when Freud points out that the avarice, the formalism and the obstinacy come from anal-erotic sources or it removes from these sources its powerful contributions.

On the other hand, it is necessary to emphasize that in 1917, Freud still studied the Wolf Man. This patient recalled certain thoughts, certain blasphemies that came to his head as an inspiration of the devil; such as the God-shit idea. According to Freud, the analysis of the faeces meaning makes clear that the obsessional thoughts that constrained the Wolf Man to relate God with the excrement had another meaning; since God-shit was the abbreviation of an offering that is eventually heard in a non-abbreviated manner as 'shit on God' or 'shit something for God' which means give him a baby or get the Wolf Man to give a baby to someone.

Therefore, the compulsion that dominated the Wolf Man to think 'God-shit', 'God-pig' is a product of a conciliation in connection with his anal eroticism. Before the analysis, the faeces had the meaning of money to the Wolf Man and the master points out that "faeces, baby and penis form so, a unity, an unconscious concept [...] throughout these association trails, the libidinal cathexis can become displaced or intensified (Freud, 1918[1914], p.92).

In addition to this triad, the obsessional structures "can be classified as desires, temptations, impulses, reflections, doubts, orders, or prohibitions" (Freud, 1909, p. 193). Remembering that the obsessional thoughts suffer a deformation similar to that which the oneiric thoughts pass before becoming the manifest content of a dream. The technique of deformation in obsessional thoughts is a deformation technique by omission or ellipse. On the ellipse, he says:

> "This technique preferably applies to jokes, but in the case of the Rats Man it worked well, as a means of avoiding that things were understood [...] the deformation technique by ellipse appears to be a characteristic of the obsessional neurosis; I have noticed this also in the obsessional thoughts of other patients" (1909, p. 107).

In the obsessional neurosis, the unconscious mental processes sometimes erupt into consciousness in its pure and undeformed way. Such incursions occur at all and any stage of the thought process; and that at the moment of these incursions, the obsessional ideas can, in most cases, be recognized as a long-term formation.

Therefore, the thought in the obsessional neurosis replaces the act and instead of the substitutive act, some thought that anticipates it perseveres with the full force of compulsion. According to Freud, "insofar as this regression of the act to the thinking becomes more marked or less market, a case of obsessional neurosis will exhibit the obsessional thought characteristics (i.e., the obsessional ideas)" (1909, p. 221).

This means that the thought process becomes sexualized since the sexual pleasure is typically connected to the thought content "and it is seen applied to the very act of thinking, and the satisfaction derived from the fact of reaching the conclusion of a line of thought is felt as a sexual satisfaction" (1909, p. 211-212). Thus, a thought process is obsessional or compulsive when in consequence of an inhibition on the motor end of the psychic system; it is performed with an expenditure of energy that is normally reserved only for the actions.

During the analysis of the Rats Man, Freud mentions some mental traits of obsessional neurotic. The Rats Man was superstitious, he believed in premonitions and in prophetic dreams. These characteristics are resumed when publishing "Totem and Taboo", when he declares that "all obsessional neurotic are so superstitions, often against their better judgment" (1913, p. 97).

In addition to the superstition, he points out that another mental need of obsessional neurotic is the need for uncertainty in their lives, or doubt. The creation of the uncertainty is one of the methods used by the neurosis to attract the patient out of reality and isolate him from the world. The predilection of obsessional neurotic by uncertainty and by doubt leads them to guide their thoughts of preference for those themes to which the all mankind is uncertain, being their knowledge and judgments exposed to doubt. For Freud (1909, p. 202), "the main topics of this nature are fatherhood, length of life, life after death, and memory". Remember that in the case of the Rats Man, "the doubt is, in fact, a doubt of his own love [...] and the compulsion, according to Freud, is an attempt for some compensation by the doubt and for a correction of intolerable inhibition conditions of which the doubt presents testimony" (1909, p. 209-210). The doubt corresponds to the internal perception that the patient has, or his own indecision, which, as a result of the inhibition of his love through his hatred, it possesses him in view of any intended action.

During the analysis of the Rats Man, Freud highlights another characteristic of the obsessional thought: the omnipotence of thoughts; a characteristic that is resumed in *Totem and Taboo* of 1913.

In *Totem and Taboo*, Freud (1913, p.97) states that "[...] the omnipotence of thought, the overvaluation of mental processes in comparison with reality, plays an unrestricted role in the emotional life of neurotic patients and everything that derives from it". It is in the obsessional neurosis that the omnipotence survival of thoughts is more clearly visible; since in this neurosis the consequences of this primitive mode of thinking are closer to consciousness. The neurotics live a world apart, where only the 'neurotic currency' is the current currency. The obsessional neurotic is only affected by what is thought with intensity and imagined with emotion, while the agreement with the *external* reality has no importance.

Regarding the thought in the obsessional neurosis, Freud points out that "with respect to the neurotic, we find that, on one hand, a considerable part of this primitive attitude survived in its constitution, and on the other, that the sexual repression that occurred with them caused a greater sexualization of their thought processes" (1913, p. 97). He compares the mental life of savages with the mental life of a neurotic. According to Freud, the omnipotence of thought is the principle that drives the magic, the technique of the animistic modality of the savages' thought. The superstitions that the obsessional neurotic practice in common life reveal the similarity of the obsessional neurotic with the savages who believe that they can change the outside world by the simple thought. He declares that the primitive men and the neurotics assign a high valuation, an overvaluation of *psychic* acts and emphasizes that "[…] it can be said that, in the primitive man, the process of thinking is still, largely, sexualized" (1913, p. 98). This is the origin of the savages and neurotics faith in the omnipotence of thoughts, of their unshakeable confidence in the possibility of controlling the world and its inaccessibility to the experiences.

Freud also draws up a relationship between the taboo and the obsessional prohibitions of neurotic. He declares that the horror to the incest presented by the savages (from Australia) reveals an agreement "with the mental life of neurotic patients" (1913, p. 37).

According to Freud, this phobia of contact present in the obsessional neurosis is the desire (unconscious) of touching that is confronted with the external prohibition against the contact realization, the touch. The prohibition cannot abolish the instinct; however, represses the desire to touch and banishes it to the unconscious. This is the characteristic of the ambivalent attitude of the neurotic individual towards the given object.

The neurotic constantly desires to touch, but the prohibition is uproariously conscious while the persistent desire to touch is unconscious and the individual knows nothing about his desire to touch. Anything that directs the thoughts of the obsessional neurotic to the forbidden object, anything that puts him in intellectual contact with the forbidden object is as prohibited as the direct physical contact.

According to Freud, the obsessional acts, the obsessional thoughts, the defensive measures, and the obsessional orders show signs of being derived from ambivalent impulses "both simultaneously corresponding to a desire and to a counter-desire, and predominantly acting in the name of the opposing trends" (1913, p. 52). The ambivalence, i.e. the opposing trends, is found in the taboos, in obsessional acts, and in obsessional thoughts.

For Freud, in the neurosis, in the root of the prohibition, there is always a hostile impulse against someone who the patient loves, i.e., a desire that this person dies. This impulse is repressed by a prohibition and this is linked to a specific act, which, by displacement, represents a hostile act against the loved person. There is a threat of death if the act is performed, but the process goes beyond and the original desire that the person dies is replaced by the fear that he could die. According to Freud, "whenever I managed to penetrate the mystery [of obsessional neurosis], I found that the expected disgrace was the death" (1913, p. 58).

But how would this ambivalence in obsessional thought occur? According to Freud, the consciousness emerges based on the emotional ambivalence; as it occurs with the taboo and the obsessional neurosis. This means that one of the opposing feelings involved is unconscious and kept under repression by the compulsive domination on the other.

About the ambivalence in neurosis, Freud resumes this issue in the article *"The Future of an Illusion"*; noting that in the protection function, the mother is replaced by the stronger father, but the child attitude with the father is nuanced by a peculiar ambivalence. The own father constitutes a danger to the child, perhaps because of the relationship prior to him with his mother. Thus, "he (the child) fears him as much as he craves him and admires him" (1927, p. 33).

This ambivalence is resumed in *Moses and the Monotheism*, almost twelve years after *The Future of an Illusion*, when

Freud resumes the ambivalence of the son by his father, he assets that "the ambivalence is part of the essence of the relationship with the father: in the course of time also the hostility could not arouse what once again propelled the sons to kill their admired and feared father" (1939, p. 159).

The obsessional thought from the second Freudian topical: a brief discussion.

To address the superego in this second moment of the Freudian work, it is convenient to remember that for Freud, in obsessional neurosis, the superego "becomes rougher, ruder and more tormented than where the development has been normal" (1926, p. 117). The too rigorous superego insists even more strongly in the suppression of sexuality, since sexuality has assumed such repellent forms in obsessional neurosis.

The ego of the obsessional neurotic, due to the obedience to the severe and rude superego, produces strong reactive formations of consciousness, piety and neatness. For Freud, these reactive formations of obsessional neurosis "are […] exaggerations of normal traits of character that are developed during the latency period" (1926, p.153). The reactive formation appears in the form of an ego change and it is performed by reinforcing the attitude that is the opposite of the instinctive trend which must be repressed like in piety, in consciousness and neatness. Therefore, in obsessional neurosis, the anti-cathexis performs a particular relevant role in the ego protection, making a reactive change in it.

About the thought in this neurosis, he says:

> "What penetrates the consciousness is, in general, only a distorted substitute that is of a vague nature […] or so caricatured that it becomes unrecognizable. Even where the repression has not usurped the contents of aggressive impulse, it certainly got

rid of its concomitant affective character. Aggressiveness seems to the ego rather an impulse, but a 'thought' that does not arouse any feelings" (1926, p. 153).

Thus, in *Inhibitions, Symptoms and Anxiety*, Freud resumes the theme of the obsessional ideas and states that, before becoming conscious; the unpleasant obsessional ideas pass through the repression process. In this process of the obsessional thought formation, Freud also highlights the isolation mechanism; since the isolation technique is peculiar to the obsessional neurosis. In the obsessional thought, the experience is not forgotten, but instead, it is destituted of his affection, and his associative connections are suppressed or interrupted so that it remains as isolated, not being reproduced in the common processes of thought.

In this text of 1926, Freud argues that the isolation technique is reproduced in the obsessional neurosis "receiving at the same time a motor reinforcement for magical purposes since the motor isolation is intended to ensure an interruption in the thought connection" (1926, p. 122). We should not forget that the ego of the obsessive has great doses of isolation work to perform in its role of guiding the thought chain. Therefore, the ego of the obsessional neurotic is more attentive and makes a more pronounced isolation in the obsessional neurosis due to the high degree of tension due to the conflict that exists between the superego and the id of the obsessive.

Conclusion

Throughout this paper, we could notice that the obsessional neurosis has a variety of characteristics in its way of thinking; since this is marked by the regression of the act for the thought. Since the *Additional Observations* Freud had already highlighted the dissociation of the affection from the obsessional idea, a dissociation that is reaffirmed in the isolation mechanism during the analysis of the Rats Man.

In the period in which he analyzed this patient, Freud writes *Character and Anal Eroticism*, where he gives huge contributions to the various forms of anality present in obsessional thought; such as the attachment to money that comes from anal-erotic sources. Furthermore, in any case of obsessional neurosis, we can find deformations in the obsessional thought arising from the omission or ellipse technique. Therefore, these thoughts express all the animism and superstition of the neurotic and the way to relate to the external environment.

In this way of thinking we can find reactive formations in the service of ambivalence, causing the taboo of touching that move the obsessions expressed by the desire of touching and the fear of touching.

The obsessional thought is the organizer of the human society; since the peculiar characteristics of obsessional neurosis are universal characteristics of human society. Thus, I conclude this paper with the wise words of the psychoanalysis father: "the obsessional neurosis is, undoubtedly, the most interesting and compensatory theme of analytical research" (1926, p. 136).

Bibliography

FREUD, S. (1894/1996). The Defense Neuropsychosis. *Brazilian Standard Edition of the Complete Works of Sigmund Freud,* vol. III, Rio de Janeiro: Imago.

FREUD, S. (1895/1996). Obsessions and Phobias. *ESB,* vol. I, Rio de Janeiro: Imago.

FREUD, S.(1896a /1996). Draft K. *ESB,* vol.I, Rio de Janeiro: Imago.

FREUD, S.(1896b/ 1996). Additional Observations about the Defense Neuropsychosis. *ESB*, vol. III, Rio de Janeiro: Imago.

FREUD, S. (1898/1996). The Sexuality in the Etiology of Neurosis. *ESB*, vol. III, Rio de Janeiro: Imago.

FREUD, S. (1907/1996). Obsessive Acts and Religious Practices. *ESB*, vol. IX. Rio de Janeiro: Imago.

FREUD, S. (1908/1996). Character and Anal Eroticism. *ESB*, vol. IX, Rio de Janeiro: Imago.

FREUD, S. (1909/1996). Notes on a case of obsessional neurosis. *ESB*, vol. X. Rio de Janeiro: Imago.

FREUD, S. (1913/ 1996). Totem andTaboo. *ESB*, vol. XIII. Rio de Janeiro: Imago.

FREUD, S. (1917/1996). The InstinctTransformationsExemplified in Anal Eroticism. *ESB*, vol. XVII, Rio de Janeiro: Imago.

FREUD, S. (1918/1996). History of an Infantile Neurosis. *ESB*, vol. XIV. Rio de Janeiro: Imago.

FREUD, S. (1926/1996). Inhibitions, Symptoms and Anxiety. *ESB*, vol. XX. Rio de Janeiro: Imago.

FREUD, S. (1927/1996). The Future of an Illusion.*ESB*, vol. XXI, Rio de Janeiro: Imago, 1996.

FREUD, S. (1939/1996). MosesandtheMonotheism. *ESB*, vol. XXIII, Rio de Janeiro: Imago.

The body image constitution

Introduction

This article seeks to focus on the neurologist Paul Schilder vision on the body image formation, based on a literature review of his work entitled *The Body Image: the psyche constructive energies*. For starting this discussion, how does Schilder understand body image?

According to Schilder (1935, p. 11) "body image is understood as the figuration of our body formed in our minds; i.e., the way the body is presented to us".

The body schema (also understood as body image) is the three-dimensional image that all people have of themselves. In this three-dimensional aspect we have the psychological, sociological and physiological aspects.

For Schilder (1935, p. 15), "when studding the body image, we should address the central psychological problem of the relation between the impressions of our senses, our movements, and the general motility". This means that the body schema is in perpetual self-construction, living in continuous differentiation and integration. On the other hand, our body postural model relates to the postural model of other bodies. Our body image experience and other bodies experience are closely interconnected. Therefore, the emotions, actions and perceptions are inseparable from our body image. They contribute to our body image construction.

Material and method

The method to be used in this article is supported in a bibliographical survey on the work entitled *The Body Image: The Psyche Constructive Energies*, published in 1935, which seeks to give prominence to the sociological and psychological aspects of body image constitution, emphasizing the erogenous zones, the libidinal phases and the social aspects throughout its constitution.

Results

First, to Schilder (1935), the body image begins to form from birth. Namely, since birth, two factors have special participation in the body image creation: one is the pain and the other is the members' motor control.

The pain helps us decide what we want to get closer to the ego and what we want to maintain the furthest possible from it. In addition, the visual experience has a leading role in the body image formation. This experience is also lived through the action. In other words, it is through the actions and determinations that we give the final shape to our body ego. Thus, the visual impressions influence the body schema, since body image can be disturbed by experimental changes in vision, but it is restructured, forming a new unit.

For Schilder (1935, p. 60) "the body schema development also occurs parallel to the motor sensory development". Throughout the psychic development, the movement leads to a better guidance in relation to our body. We do not know much about the body, unless we move it. The movement is an important factor of unification of our body different parts and through it we come to a definite relationship with the outside world and with the objects, and only through the contact with the outside that we become able to correlate the various impressions about our body. The knowledge of our body depends, in large part, of our own action. Thus, since birth, the body postural model needs to be built. It is a creation and a construction, the production of a shape. The structuring process is only possible when it closely relates with the world experiences.

For Schilder (1935, p. 102) "the body image, in its result, is a unit. But this unit is not rigid, but liable of transformation. And all the senses are always contributions to the body scheme creation". In other words, the visual perceptions strongly influence the body image. The images change under the impulses and motor imagination influences. Schilder (1935) argues that these distortions are called metamorphosias. Among these, we have polyopia that would be the tendency to multiply the visual image, becoming larger (macropsia) or smaller (micropsia)

The Libidinal Structure of Body Image

Schilder uses the psychoanalytic theory to explain the libidinal structure of body image.

In his understanding of the psychoanalytic work, Schilder (1935, p. 107) points out that "we are interested in our body integrity". He claims that the libido belongs to our own body. He declares that, in principle, libido is given to the body as a whole. This is the narcissistic stage. In this phase, the child only cares for herself. This stage, referred to as primary narcissism, is followed by an autoerotic phase, in which the libido is focused on body parts that have special erogenous signification. Concomitantly to auto-eroticism, Schilder describes the pre-genital and child genital phases.

The first phase or would be oral phase. In this, the milk intake occurs and the erogenous zone is the mouth. At this phase, the body tries to incorporate the outside world, which is only considered according to its ability to produce (or not) satisfaction. At this point, the child also enjoys the sensations from the skin. There is a cutaneous eroticism.

In the oral phase, aggression can also occur aiming to destroy the mother breast. This aggressiveness (and consequently, the sadism) can persist in the anal phase.

The second phase is the anal-sadistic phase. In this there is pleasure in defecation and the erogenous zone is the anus. During this phase, the outside world receives an interest portion from the child, occurring anal and homosexual tendencies in relation to external objects.

The third phase would be the phallic, which coincides with the Oedipus Complex (nuclear complex of the psychic subject constitution). At this phase, the genitals acquire a new meaning and become the main libidinal zone in the body. At this phase, there is a complete understanding of the child's body as something opposite to the outside world. After the end of the Oedipus complex, we have the secondary narcissism aspect, a moment when the libido is withdrawn from "outside world".

According to Schilder reading, narcissism is seen as a large (libidinal) reservoir which lends part of its contents to the objects. The energy that was withdrawn from this reservoir can be brought back at any time. And what is the relationship between the primary narcissism and the body image? For Schilder (1935), any libido or energy of ego desires can only appear in connection with an object. We are in a world, and the objects are part of it. When we live, we are facing this world. There is always a person and this person attitude. An attitude is an attitude to something: the narcissistic libido object is the body image. But there is no doubt that our body can only exist as part of the world.

For the newborn, body and world are interconnected experiences. One is not possible without the other. In so primitive level, the boundary between body and world is not clearly defined. It will be easier to perceive a part of the body in the world than a part of the world in the body. Thus, the body will be projected in the world, and this will be introjected in the body. And in adulthood, body and world are in constant exchange.

Thus, at birth there is a zone of lack of differentiation between body and world. But the body image must be developed and built. Libido is linked to the different parts of body image and, in various phases of libido development, the body model will continuously change.

In the body scheme, overall structure, the erogenous zones will have a leading role. In other words, we can assume that the body image, during the oral phase of development, will be centered in the mouth and, in anal phase, in the anus. The libidinal flow of energy will greatly influence the body image. And during the body image construction, there will be a continuous interaction between ego and id.

Erogenous Zones of Body Image

For Schilder (1935, p. 142) "the own organs [of the body] force the individual to a continuous contact with the outside world, and there is no doubt that, at least in part, we discover our body through these contacts". The enormous psychological importance of every orifice of the body is present since birth. Through the mouth we eat the food. Andin adulthood, by means of certain cavities we eject urine, sexual products, faeces and air. In addition, the body surface is also an erogenous zone. The skin is easily irritable and, consequently, it is an irritation organ. There are continuous sensations that lead the child to touch or make people around him touch his skin.

It is very important to note that much of the body is discovered by the hands. In addition to the hand and look, the contact with the others (fathers, mothers, friends and neighbors) and the interest that these demonstrate to the various parts of our body will be of huge importance for the development of the body postural model; since "whenever a part of our body image receives excessive importance, the symmetry and the internal balance of body image are destroyed" (Schilder, 1935, p. 113). Therefore, the organic pain (that leads the body model libidinal structure to change immediately), the organic diseases, the erogenous zones, our hands action on the body, the others actions regarding our body, the others interest by our body are important factors for the body image final structuring.

In addition, the libidinal structures differences reflect in the body postural model structure. Individuals in whom a partial desire is increased will feel a certain point of the body, the particular erogenous zone belonging to the desire, in the center of his body images, as if the energy was accumulated in certain points. There are energy lines connecting different erogenous zones and we will have variations in the body image structuring, according to the individual psychosexual tendencies.

For Schilder (1935, p. 159) "every erogenous zone has typical extension lines". In adulthood, there is the extension of these erogenous zones to certain parts of the body. The anal zone extends to the back. The mouth, usually, extends to the interior plan. In other words, extends to the hands, mouth and nose inner part. Therefore, it is impossible to study the libidinal structure of body image in isolation. It is an integral part of the individual internal vital history and, to understand it, it is necessary to study the libidinal development since childhood. Thus, our body knowledge is developed based on the continuously renewed contact with the outside world since childhood, and the body image construction is based not only on the person individual story, but also in his relations with others.

For Schilder (1935, p. 164) "the body schema is a unit that not only incorporates parts of the outside world, but also waives these. There is not only a tendency to structure the body postural model, but also to destroy this image". For example, when we eat food or drink, something from outside world is added to body image. After digestion, the intestinal movement just physically separates faeces from body, but psychologically, these continue to be part of us.

The anatomical configuration (of genital organs) plays an important role in body structure. A protuberance belongs less to the body; because whenever a body part connects less closely with the rest, there is a fear of losing it. It is the fear for body integrity, which is based on the postural model internal qualities.

In addition, the body postural model only remains stable for a short time, immediately changing. Probably, the psychic life figurations instability only connotes a passing phase with which the next phase can be contrasted. But there is no doubt that, in our psychic life, there are always tendencies to form units. But whenever a unit, a Gestalt is created, this immediately tends to change and destroy. Destruction is a partial phase of construction, which is a project and life general characteristic. Destroy to rebuild a new image.

Discussion:
Libidinal Development of Body Image

Schilder, in his reading of Freudian work, points out that since the beginning of life there a nucleus of body image in the oral zone. Using Berfeld, Schilder (1935) admits that there is a primary development that begins in the oral zone and a secondary refinement that differentiates the body ego from the outside world. So, he points out:

"We have reasons to believe that there is an internal development, a maturation in all fields of psychic life, and that there are internal factors in the organism relatively independent of the experiences that determine this evolution. The maturation process acquires its final form from the individual experiences, which will depend, largely, on the vital experience, training and emotional activities" (SCHILDER, 1935, p. 179).

Our body image is not always the same. The body image evolution is, somewhat, parallel to the perceptions, thoughts and object relations development.

Every desire and every libidinal trend change immediately the body image structure. In any attitude, we desire to modify the postural model or body scheme spatial relationship. The minute we see something, muscular actions start leading to changes in its perception. All impulse or desire modifies the body image, its gravity and its mass. Thus, in every action and every desire we intend to obtain a body image change.

For Schilder "the body image can shrink or expand, can give its parts to outside world or seize upon parts of it" (1935, p. 176). For example, the lips and face painting, hair discoloration and tattoo are attempts to change the body image. The meaning of all these changes of appearance is not always conscious; because there is a symbolic meaning, as for example, the skin cleaning can be considered an example of impulse to overcome unconscious anal tendencies.

In addition to hygiene, clothes became a part of body image. That is, any piece of clothes dressed becomes, immediately, part of the body image.

As the clothes are part of the body schema, these gain the same sense of body parts and can represent various symbolic meanings. Consequently, all transformations found in body image can be found in the clothes. This means that clothes can become a means to entirely change our body image; and when imitating a famous person's clothes, we modify our postural image, incorporating others image. Therefore, the body images are not isolated entities. The body images community is the basis of all social function.

It is necessary to emphasize that body image passes through a continuous process of expansion and reduction. The primitive peoples and certain psychotic patients can modify body image through a simple process of libidinal imagination; for example, they transform an individual into a werewolf on the basis of their beliefs. People already considered 'neurotic' only achieve minor "autoplastic" modifications through masks and clothes.

Humans are surrounded and curtailed by their body images. One of the reasons for the transformation and use of clothes is the desire to overcome the rigidity of body image, which can be transformed through paintings, jewelry etc.

The body can also be modified as a whole. We can make holes in the body or insert metal or wood pieces in it, as it occurred with the primitive peoples.

According to Schilder "one can also try to modify the body image in a less violent way, through all kinds of gymnastics" (1935, p. 179). So, the dance and gymnastics are ways to decrease the body postural model rigid shape. The dance leads to a disruption and a change of body image, leading us from a body image change to a psychic attitude change.

For Schilder (1935), we expand and contract the body postural model, we remove and add parts, we rebuild it; we mix details; create new details; we do this with our body and with its own expression. There is a construction and a destruction linked to the needs, conflicts and energy of the total personality. During the construction and destruction phases appear two basic human tendencies. One is the tendency to crystallize unities and ensure rest points, immutability and absence of change. The other is the tendency to obtain a continuous flow, a permanent change.

Beauty and Body Image

For Schilder "a beauty should be related to body postural model. When we consider the human figure beauty, we immediately realize that the aesthetic interest certainly relates closely with the interest in sex" (1935, p. 128). The human being beauty does not cause the desires immediately, but it brings inside the seeds of desires development, since the human figure beauty has a direct relation with sexuality.

Beauty is a social phenomenon. The human body, its postural model, is the first object of plastic arts and painting. The beauty object causes sexual impulses without satisfying them; but, at the same time, allows everyone to enjoy it. The beauty is, also, giving up your own claims to the benefit of all.

It is obvious that the aesthetic influence disappears when sexual desire becomes stronger. We concluded that the aesthetic object triggers instinctual attitudes, but such attitudes are prematurely inhibited and interrupted, so that the aesthetic pleasure, although it offers rest and relaxation, it does not allow a complete satisfaction of desires. Thus, this pleasure continues far from the ideal to be achieved.

The aesthetic object offers a promise and a semi-satisfaction of desires, and such desires are characterized as incompletely satisfied and unfinished by the fact that, in the aesthetic figure, more than a desire seeks expression and satisfaction.

The aesthetic effect consists in the fact that instinctive attitudes are caused, but not developed. That is, the aesthetic experiences are incomplete and can never be completed. The aesthetic object acquires its color when impounding the instinctive energy. The person who appreciates aesthetic experience enjoys the free movement of his desires, without assuming the appropriate responsibility for it.

For Schilder (1935), we should not underestimate the importance of beauty and ugliness in human life. Beauty can be a promise of complete satisfaction or a way to get such satisfaction. Our own beauty or ugliness does not take into account only the image that we have of ourselves, but also the image the others build about us, and which we will take back. Thus, the body image is the result of social life.

Certainly, beauty and ugliness are not isolated individual phenomena, but social phenomena of greater importance. Our own body image and that of others, their beauty or ugliness, become the basis of our sexual and social activities.

For Schilder "the beauty concept is directly related to each people culture" (1935, p. 235). The beauty standard is always the libidinal expression of a society, such as the deformation practices adopted in the primitive societies.

When we structure the individual and others body image, we always tend to build something static that soon will be dissolved again. We always return to the body primary positions. When we think of a person running, we see him changing from a primary position to another primary position. That is, the primary positions are the relative rest position, the moment that the movement is not considered, but yes the postural model crystallized unit.

We should realize that our and others body image is not just a body image at rest, but a body image in motion. But the beauty is especially connected with the body image at rest, with the cover images of certain fashion magazines. And that is why we are so surprised when seeing an isolated phase of a movement in an old photograph

The body image three-dimensionality

Schilder (1935) considers the body as a unit, but points out that to understand the body image, we must consider the three-dimensional aspect: the world, the body and the mind. He says: "it would be wrong to try to dissolve them in a cluster of isolated parts. We have three categories [...] of world, body and personality" (1935, p. 246).

In the construction of body image, it is essential the contact with the external reality, because all experiences with external reality already modify the most primitive body image imaginable. Parts of these experiences are accepted or not. Thus, the body image is continuously built through levels and layers, taking into consideration past and present experiences (such as memory and learning).

For Schilder "to build the body image, we need to know where are the different members of our body" (1935, p. 249). The body postural model, the members' knowledge and their mutual relations are necessary to start any movement.

The body postural model finds its expression clearer in the phantom members of people who have lost their members more or less abruptly. An attitude regarding the phantom member shows that people affected with the loss of a member wish to recreate the body integrity. Certain experiments and observations of amputated people show that they contain in themselves the amputated member phantom.

The postural model is modified to each object that touches the body. This model also has relation with the postural model of people around us. In addition, the emotional life has an important role in the final form of body postural model, as it will change the relative value and the clarity of the various parts of the body image, according to the libidinal tendencies.

This change may be a surface change, but also an internal body change. The libidinal structure is expressed in the emphasis given to the different parts of postural model and in appearances resulting from its shapes. What happens in one part of the body can be transposed to another. That is, the female sexual organ cavity can appear as cavity in other parts of the body. The male sexual organ can be represented by earrings, piercings in other parts of the body.

Schilder (1935) calls this a transposition from a body region to another. Therefore, a part of the body can symbolize another part, such as the nose can take the importance of the phallus. Any protruding part can become a symbol of the male sexual organ. The body cavities and orifices can be exchanged by each other freely. The vagina, anus, mouth, ears, and even the nose cavities belong to the same group of orifices.

Conclusion

We elaborate our body image according to the experiences gain through the actions and attitudes, as well as by words or acts directed to our body. In addition, the others attitudes towards their own bodies will also have a major influence on our body image.

We can take other people's body parts and incorporate them into our body image. This is called personalization. Thus, the identification of the group where this subject is inserted, the projection of individual fantasies to the outside world, and the personalization have a prominent role in the construction of an individual body image.

In addition to these three aspects, Schilder (1935) also points out that libidinal conflicts constantly change body image. There is a tendency to keep the body image within its bounds, and another to expand and extend it. There is also a tendency to keep their parties united and dissipate them all over the world. So, the movement and the expression belong to destructive phases in the continuous process of changes in the body postural model.

Based on this work, it can be concluded that the erotic changes in body image are always a social phenomenon, and followed by the corresponding phenomena in the body image of others. There is a constant exchange between parts of our own body image and the parts of others body image. This means that there is a projection and a personalization. But the others body image totality o (such as friends and neighbors) can be taken in the identification with them; as well as the totality of our body image can be projected to outside.

Therefore, a discussion on body image as an isolated entity is necessarily incomplete. A body is always the expression of an ego, of a personality, and it is inserted into a world. Even a preliminary response to the body problem cannot be given, unless we try a preliminary response on the personality and the world. In other words, for a body image study, any researcher is expected to give prominence to the psychological, physiological and sociological aspects of body image; i.e., its three-dimensionality.

Bibliographical Reference

SCHILDER, Paul (1935/1994). *The Body Image: The Psyche Constructive Energies.* Translation of Rosanne Wertman. São Paulo: Martins Fontes.

The Hysteria: from the Freudian divan to the present days

The hysteria: yesterday and today

Among the classes of neurosis studied by Sigmund Freud, the conversion hysteria can be considered the hysterical neurosis itself. This neurosis is side by side to the obsessional neurosis and the anxiety hysteria – the phobia – which wealth was 'hushed up' by the famous Panic Syndrome.

Among these three classes of neurosis – the obsessive, phobic and the hysterical -, the conversion hysteria was the precursor to the psychoanalysis origin. In his early studies, Freud did not use the 'conversion hysteria terminology, since the 'conversion' terminology was considered as a hysteria itself. In this conversion, the psychic impulse, interlaced to the desire, is bodily manifested through contractions, blindness and other symptoms, but it was on the analysis of a phobia case – the little Hans – that the father of psychoanalysis began to discern between the anguish hysteria (with all its clinical richness that the famous psychiatry confined it) and the conversion hysteria.

In the thresholds of this historical trajectory, between the pre-psychoanalysis and the analysis of little Hans, the conversion hysteria and its clinical manifestations were never relegated to a second plan. In this historic meander, the historian Roudinesco (1988) points out that, between 1880 and 1900, the world was going through a real epidemic of hysterical symptoms, being these understood by doctors, historians and writers as the convulsive signs of female nature as a result of the industrial society consequence in the 19th century.

This time Jean Martin Charcot is highlighted, a French physician and neurologist, who understood the hysteria as a functional and hereditary disease, which affected men and women. Through the hypnosis, he tried to demonstrate his assumptions on this pathology.

This technique was widely used with his patients of Salpêtrière, inducing to his hysterical symptoms. This doctor, to whom Freud had a huge consideration, directly influenced the psychoanalysis father understandings on hysteria. Between 1888 and 1893, Freud brings from Charcot the idea in which the hysterical neurosis is a result of a childhood trauma, reporting that his would have its sexual causes and would be the result of a sexual abuse lived by the child during his childhood.

Due to his self-analysis in 1897, he waives this theory and emphasizes the role of fantasy in the hysteria etiology. In the passage to the 20th century, the psychoanalysis technique suffers a new change: Freud abandons the cathartic method of Breuer - a method which psychoanalytic therapy was based on the treatments carried out by hypnosis. In this method, through hypnosis, the patient encountered the traumatic events, releasing the emotions related to him.

In contrast, Freud adopts the free association, focusing the verbalized material freely throughout the sessions. This method, according to Laplanche (2001), would insist in indiscriminately expressing the thoughts freely from the childhood memories, reports of dreams and the symptoms brought by the patient.

At the turn of the century, in 1900, Freud writes *The Dreams Interpretation*, the book which is considered the landmark of the beginning of psychoanalysis. In this context, hysteria was understood as a psychic conflict and no longer as a result of a traumatic event. There the hypnosis had been abandoned and the free association method gains its space.

Before proceeding, I would like to highlight that, although 114 years have passed from the hypnosis technique abandonment, this, in our Brazilian current society, gains space between charlatan 'professionals', which use it in favor of their primitive religious rituals. We are no longer in Salpêtrière and the hysterics are no longer put on stage; but the stage was transformed into the television and the internet, which give room for the collective alienation that moves a mass in the search of an answer to the others suffering. A reply in the search for nothing, moved by the desire; such as the primitives that beat their drums in the search for an answer from their loved superior for the pain of their soul. Therefore, we observe the suffering of a mass in which many, by the scientific ignorance, put, often, the salvation in people who they shamelessly use, and without the ethical pillar, the distortions of hypnosis technique to justify the failures and the diseases of this crowd, evoking the evil beings within these people. So, we return to middle ages, because all that is wrong is not our fault, but the punishments of superior beings that we should exorcise.

In this meander, hysteria never was made so clamored in our society. But before proceeding, I would like to point out that we cannot equate hysteria to madness, like many still do, repeating the mistakes of our past. I hear many saying that the hysteric is a crazy woman that screams, kicks and shows up. But it is not. On the contrary, if the show occurs, this is of her own desire that circulates and moves the dissatisfaction of her own psychism. So, if hysteria puts in evidence the desire and we owe them the psychoanalysis origin, we will return to Freud, specifically until 1901, when Freud wrote the classic case of hysteria: *the Dora case.*

In this clinical case, he considered hysteric "any person in which an opportunity of sexual excitement provokes [...]a sensation of disgust, whether that person presents or not somatic symptoms" (1901, p. 50). However, it was after the studies on infant sexuality that Freud indicated the core of hysterical neurosis: this would be in the impossibility to liquidate the Oedipus complex (nuclear complex of the psychic subject constitution). Such statement requires a better explanation.

All of us, human beings, entered in the Oedipus complex, but how each one dealt with the destinations of this complex only an analysis can point out. In this meander, according to the Freudian theory, the female Oedipus complex does not occur similar to the male, since in the female path of this complex, the penis envy comes to perform a key role. In this case, the girl enters this complex by the discovery that not all feature a male organ. In this turmoil, she disconnects from the mother – since this deprived her from the male organ – In the search of her father, expressing the desire to have a son with him, which in the past she desired to have from her mother. Thus, all female Oedipus complex entire development is concrete in the penile envy shadow. However, it is the fear of the maternal love loss that throws the girl 'out' of this complex, and the girl may show three possible escapes: the sexual inhibition or hysteria, the masculinity complex and the femininity.

As the female hysteria is presented as possible it exists to the female Oedipus complex, it is the libidinal fixation in the phallic phase that will move it in its eternal complaints of dissatisfaction. In other words, among the three phases of psychosexual development described by Freud – the oral, anal and phallic – the hysteria features a great part of the libidinal fixation in the phallic phase, a phase that culminates with the Oedipus complex. In contrast, if this phallic fixation was not enough, there is also a small fixation on oral phase, which justifies why many hysterical have such strong melancholic traits. Therefore, it was this world so rich and enigmatic of female universe that surprised Freud at each phase of his work.

However, I point out that every hysterical will move according to these fixations, assuming, in each case, a unique position against its transference. So, the psychotherapists are responsible for hearing them, always being attentive of their fantasies (and not the reality) in their verbalizations.

Those fantasies that launch new light on the manifestations of its libidinal fixations: each hysterical move by the phallus (or its lack), leading her to claim prominent places and positions in society, putting in checkmate the male positions and jobs. This means that the hysterical complaint, which reflects this phallic position and that still moves many women, is very common when they assume roles and positions below the men. Such difference can never end, because it is this what drives her desire, given the lack. And in the completeness pursuit of this lack, a fact that she can never show, the hysterical is capable of great facets, these being of great social recognition.

Here I would like to point out a book called *Everything in Pink*, written by the own hands of the arts godmother of São Paulo, the great Yolanda Penteado. In my understanding, this author, while describes her own story, brings the issue of love of her childhood in relation to her parents, as well as the good identificatory relation with her mother, pointing to the life force that was present in her psychic constitution. When getting aware of her love frustrations and how she stood up in view of her personal conflicts, Yolanda portrays how love and seduction were part of her daily life. To compensate this lack of phallus, she lived directly with phallic men, such as Santos Dumont (to whom she refused numerous times the marriage invitation), but came to marry, after her divorce, with Ciccillo Matarazzo, one of the Brazil's most influential men in the 50s. In the 1920 and 1930 decades, she was present in the female claims for the equal vote, since this was a right only of men. She was also present, with Anita Malfatti and Tarsila Amaral, in the Modern Art week, in the decade of 1920. Let us see: influential women that made history; but her greatest wealth was the MASP – Art Museum of São Paulo – opened in the decade of 1950. Thus, her life was marked by works that brought the phallic glow to her person. A bright that was portrayed with plenty of life in the book mentioned above.

Examples aside, I would like to return to a point of hysteria: The body symptoms. Roudinesco (1998) points out that the originality of this neurosis lies in the fact that her unconscious psychic conflicts are expressed from a theatrical way through body symbolizations, such as the attacks or convulsion in epileptic appearance, paralysis, contractures and other symptoms. Among these, a feature that catches my attention is the seduction, moved by the desire.

In hysteria, due to the phallic fixation, a triangulation is formed, where many serious hysterical are put as the third in the relationship. When they are called by the partner to assume a serious relationship, as a couple, such pleasure is lost. Consequently, the desire starts to move in search of relationships that refer again to this triangulation, decoding its identificatory problematic. I remember a hysterical saying: "I was not born to be a woman; I was born to be a lover, the other, only that". Such relationships put in evidence the rivalry with the mother in the search of the father and that, in the adulthood, it is incorporated, respectively, by the lover and the lover wife. Therefore, the seduction becomes the main weapon, but falling in its claws is everything that the hysterical least wants, but desires. And in this psychic conflict, hysteria moves in the meanders of modern society.

Due to this, the popular judgments label them of numerous derogatory names, repeating the lack of knowledge about this pathology. If before, the hysteria was decoded as demonic possession, since the witches put in checkmate the male phallus and the religion phallus, currently, the hysteria acquires even more force, because the hysterical dispute the society hypocrites' pillars through the pan protests in public square, but her demands for better wages, etc. The inquisition of fires no longer exists, but they are burned in the inquisitions that exist within each one of us when we contest what cannot be contested: the female independence. That is why this neurosis will never be outdated.

Bibliographical Reference

FREUD, S. (1900/1996). The Dreams Interpretation. *ESB*, vol. V, Rio de Janeiro: Imago.

FREUD, S. (1901/1996). Fragment of the Analysis of a Hysteria Case. *ESB*, vol. VII.Rio de Janeiro: Imago.

FREUD, S. (1923/1996). The Infant Genital Organization: an Interpolation of Sexuality Theory. *ESB*, vol. XIX, Rio de Janeiro:Imago.

FREUD, S. (1925/1996). Some Psychic Consequences of Anatomical Distinction Between the Sexes. *ESB*, vol. XIX, Rio de Janeiro:Imago.

FREUD, S. (1926/1996). Inhibitions, Symptoms and Anxiety. *ESB*, vol. XX, Rio de Janeiro:Imago.

FREUD, S.(1933/1996). XXXIII Conference - Femininity. *ESB*, vol. XXII, Rio de Janeiro:Imago.

LAPLANCHE, J. & PONTALIS, J-B.(1967/2001). *Psychoanalysis Vocabulary.* São Paulo: Martins Fontes.

PENTEADO, Yolanda (1976). *Everything in Pink.* Rio de Janeiro: Nova Fronteira.

ROUDINESCO, Elisabeth & PLON, Michel (1998). *Psychoanalysis Dictionary.* Rio de Janeiro: Jorge Zahar editor.

Ambivalent manifestations in the neurotic symptom etiology

Introduction

From the psychotherapeutic care with obsessive patients, this article aims to elucidate a reasoning about the doubt symptom in obsessional neurosis. In other words, does the doubt symptom have any relation with the anal-sadistic phase in the obsessional neurotic cared in a small public health center in the countryside of the State of São Paulo?

To answer this question, I chose a patient that I consider to be an obsessional neurotic. This patient, who I identify with the fictitious name of Paulo, seeks psychotherapy due to the ruminant thoughts of his father death (and his father had died two years before), and he also complained a lot of chest pains.

Material and method

From a clinical data survey about Paulo history, a review on the Freudian work is prepared on the anal-sadistic phase concept for the further analysis of this symptom.

It should be highlighted that, as this article is from my thesis studies on the obsessional neurosis identificatory problematic, this case publishing was approved by PUC-SP Ethics Committee, by means of protocol 173/2011.

Results

During my first contacts with this patient, I seek to understand his complaint. In his associations, he says that the chest pain and the ambulance sirens trigger compulsive thoughts of death, and this reminds him of the time he took his father to the doctor. Throughout his history narration, I realized that the paternal identification 'permeated' all this patient complaints. The alleged heart attack pains give room for complaints of intestinal pains. According to his 'concealed' memories, since the early childhood he suffered of 'trapped gases', as he himself said.

From this symptomatic complaint, I seek to listen a little more about his childhood. All and every analyst is, according to Freud (1937), "in the search of a portrait of the patient's forgotten years that is equally trustworthy and, in all essential aspects, complete [...]" (p. 276). Thus, this 'mind archeologist' service is essential for understanding Paulo libidinal and identificatory history. This reconstruction allows a better understanding of his symptomatic structuring.

Paulo, when addressing the relationship with his parents in childhood, shows a very interesting expression of how the relationship with the parental figures is structured, saying: "my brothers went away and it was left to me [...]". About his childhood, he says: "I had a lot of contact with my mother and with my father who worked. My older brother never worked with him, but he is also a shopkeeper today. I did not have much contact with him, and the little that is told is that I fought a lot with my brothers when I was a kid [...]". His other earliest memories also date back to the age of six. At this age, he had a piggy bank where he kept the coins. Since that time, he went fishing with his gather, who was much older.

When he was seven, he already attended school and remembered his third sister flirts. At that time, between seven and eight years of age, the compulsive doubts arose in the school environment. According to Paulo: "I was not a bad student. This time, I did not understand Portuguese. I had to retake tests. I had a teacher who wrote with both hands. I had a Portuguese teacher named Sandra who marked me. She was very angry. I trembled in front of her". In his associations, Paulo speaks about this teacher: "connect her with my third sister? I think these are different situations. I was afraid of her. She ordered me to look in the dictionary and I was the first, but I never understood these proparoxytones [...]. Because of my doubts, I messed everything. The proparoxytones did not come to my mind. In mathematics, I was excellent. In Portuguese, I struggled and she failed me. This teacher insisted so much on the proparoxytones that until today I do not understand it. I did two years of the fifth grade. After that, I was always the best student [...]. Everything I have done in my whole live I was in doubt. I was always suspicious. I did things with doubt and it did not work [...]".

I noticed that the doubts referred to male and female figures, such as the boss, the teacher, the son and the psychotherapist, demonstrating the ambivalence stuck in his paternal and maternal imagos. For example, at the end of the sessions, he raises several questions, such as: "do you think I did right or wrong, doctor?" So, I always try to return him the same question, not replying his demand.

Since the end of his childhood and early adolescence, he had many intestinal pains and problems with intestinal gases, which intensified at the age of seventeen. During the psychotherapy, he had several complaints due to abdominal pains caused by these gases. Every time that he could not verbalize any word that required certain tone of aggressiveness, the gases appeared. After mentioning, in several sessions, these pains, he said: "when I started putting out this volcano that was asleep through the mouth, the gases are better. Before I kept it, today I already can speak at the right time. The gases even disappeared [...]".

Thus, it is worth noting the ambivalence movement that he shows due to these abdominal pains. When he started putting these gases out, I noticed that he was less contained, listened and absorbed more my interventions. In a session, in the first year of psychotherapy, he says: "[...] I am calm today. Everything was like I expected [...]". When something goes beyond his control, he gets totally 'contained', as he said: "last week I had a momentary relapse. The idea of heart attach returned and the chest pain [...]. And these gases did not pass. It did not go out up or under. I need to relieve myself and here is the only place I can place myself [...]". Interestingly, the old heart attack fear, a thought that plagued him due to his father's death by heart attack, begins to give room to abdominal pain. An expression that specifies this movement well is when he says: "if I cannot release my volcano underneath, today I can release it through the mouth. After I started talking about things that I think, these pains began to disappear [...]. Here is a place where I can calmly talk. You listen to me. But not at home. My son does not listen to me and I do not like it [...]".

The issue of the time and people control is very strong in the dynamics of Paulo. In one session, he says: "I wonder if I am making mistakes monitoring my son? I am in a conflict. I protect my daughter-in-law, I protect her, I do not think it is right that women call my son. I checked the calls on his cell phone and there were a lot of women calls. Did I do the right thing? [...]". Regarding the time, I notice that he never delayed in any session. Time is like "gold, a great gift" for Paulo, as he says: "I have the right to 30 minutes, and not 29 minutes [...]".

Therefore, from these data brought by this patient, I would resort to the anal-sadistic phase described by Freud, once I find support on it for the understanding of this patient's uncertainties.

The anal-sadistic phase according to the Freudian theory

For Freud, the second pre-genital organization is the anal-sadistic which dominant erogenous zone is the anal. In this organization:

> The intestinal contents [...] have for the breastfeeding other important senses. It is obviously treated as a part of his own body, representing the first 'gift'. When disposing of it, the little creature can express docility to the environment surrounding him, and when refusing it, his stubbornness (Freud, 1905, p. 176).

During the anal-sadistic organization, the faeces represent the first gift that the child can give someone that he likes, demonstrating his obedience. If he denies giving the faeces, he is expressing his stubbornness.

Freud (1905) explains that "the fecal mass retention, at first intentionally practiced to take advantage of the masturbatory stimulation of the anal zone [...] is, by the way, one of the constipation reasons, which is so frequent in neuropaths" (p.176). The fecal mass retention during childhood may be related to masturbatory stimulation of anal zone, as he can also be demonstrating his pertinacity in the relationship with the people who take care of this child. And when growing, this game of retaining faeces may be symbolically present in the special scatological rituals, in ceremonial acts and similar acts which are carefully kept confidential by the neurotic individual.

According to Freud:

> Intestinal catarrhs in the early age leave child 'nervous' [...]. Children who take advantage of the anal zone erogenous stimulus are denounced by retaining the faeces until its accumulation causes violent muscular contractions and, on the passage through the anus, it may exercise an intense stimulation in the

mucosa. With that, they might produce themselves voluptuousness sensations besides the painful sensations (1905, p. 175).

During the anal-sadistic organization, it is very common that intestinal disorders provoke intense excitations in the anal zone. In infant intestinal catarrhs, the boy can come to feel pleasure in erogenous stimulation while retaining the fecal mass. In the later neurotic illness, these catarrhs that caused the anal zone stimulation influence on neurosis somatic manifestation.

Freud (1917) states that, during the first years of life, "faeces are the first gift of the child, a part of his body that he only will give to someone he loves, to whom, in fact, he will make a spontaneous offer as a sign of affection" (p. 139). The act of defecating offers the first opportunity for the child to choose between a narcissistic attitude and an attitude of object love. In this way, or he shares his faeces in the name of his love or he retains it with the purpose of autoerotic satisfaction.

Freud (1918) still postulates that "the act of ceding the faeces in favor of someone becomes a prototype of castration" (p. 89). That is, the act of providing the faeces to who he loves is the first moment in which the boy shares a piece of his own body with the purpose of obtaining the favors of anyone else.

According to Freud (1933) "the old interest in faeces becomes the great value granted to gold and money, but it also contributes to the baby and penis affective cathexis" (p. 103). The interest for the money is taken from anal-erotic sources, since the commitment on defecation disappears in later phases of adult life, emerging the interest in the money that was not present in childhood. The interest for the money enables the transfer of the primitive impulse to this new object. Therefore, the old libidinal interest for the faeces can move in adulthood, becoming the value granted to gold and money. And this same interest contributes to the baby and penis affective cathexis.

About the baby and penis affective cathexis, Freud still asserts:

> In the unconscious products – spontaneous ideas, fantasies and symptoms – the faeces concepts (money, gift), baby and penis then form a unity, an unconscious concept [...]. Throughout these association trails, the libidinal cathexis can become displaced or intensified (1917, p. 136).

The libido deposited in the faeces can displace to the penis and baby cathexis, because faeces, baby and penis "are three solid bodies; all three, forcing penetration or expulsion, stimulate a membranous passage [...]" (Freud, 1917, p. 141). That is, the libidinal cathexis of these three elements can displace or intensify, since they are symbolically equivalent and one replaces the other.

Freud (1913) points out that in anal-sadistic organization "the genital zones primacy has not yet been established". On the contrary, the instinct components that dominate this pre-genital organization of sexual life are the anal-eroticism and the sadistic" (p. 345).

In a note added in 1915 to *Three Essays*, Freud (1905) recognizes that in this organization "the division into opposites that pervades the sex life is already constituted, but they still cannot be called male and female, but rather active and passive" (p.187). In the anal-sadistic organization, the present activity is the domination impulse through the body muscles and as a passive sexual target organ, the intestine erogenous mucosa is found. At this infantile psychosexuality constitution phase, the primacy of the genital zone is not established yet. The antithesis between male and female do not exist, but rather the opposition between active and passive.

About the anal eroticism present in the anal-sadistic organization, Freud states:

> An accentuation of this anal eroticism in the pre-genital organization phase leaves behind a significant predisposition to homosexuality, in men, when the following phase of sexual function, the genital organs primacy, is reached. The manner in

which this last phase is erected on the precedent, and the concomitant remodeling of libidinal cathexis, provide the analytical
research the most interesting problems (1913, p. 346).

During this pre-genital organization, the active inclination is filled by the domain common instinct that Freud calls
sadism and the passive inclination is fueled by the anal eroticism. A fortification of anal eroticism allows an inclination to
homosexuality in males when the genitals primacy is achieved.

On Laplanche and Pontalis reading, the anal-sadistic phase
"is the first phase in which the activity-passivity polarity is
constituted. Freud makes the activity with sadism and passivity match with anal eroticism, and assigns to each of the corresponding partial impulses a different source: anal muscles and
mucosa" (2001, p. 186).

In his book, *Psychoanalytic Theory of Neurosis*, Fenichel declares that:

> Anal eroticism always has bisexual character: the anus is, at
> the same time, the organ that actively expels and a hollow organ,
> possible to stimulate by any object that enters it [...]. The objec-
> tive of female desires of male obsessive neurotic is [...] the desire
> that something is inserted or retained in his body (1981, p. 259).

On *New Conferences* published in 1932/1933, Freud highlights that the "attitude towards the libido organization phases
has changed a little [...]. Whereas, previously, it was mainly emphasized the way how each phase passed before the next phase,
our attention, now, is directed to the facts that shows how much
of each prior phase continues in the subsequent configurations
[...] (1933, p. 102).

Namely, the predominance of one phase in relation to the
other does not occur so suddenly, but gradually, since parts of
the previous organization always coexist side by side with the
latest. These sadistic impulses (which already begin during the

emergence of the teeth in the oral phase) become common in anal-sadistic phase and for being the satisfaction sought in aggression and in the excretory function. During this phase, the aggressive impulses are present, because in sadism there is an instinctive fusion of libidinal and purely destructive impulses.

Freud explains that the anal-sadistic organization "can be preserved for the entire life and permanently attract for it a good portion of sexual activity [...]. It is proper in it that the impulses opposite pairs are developed in a roughly equal manner, in a state of things described by the convenient designation of "ambivalence". (1905, p. 187). Thus, the ambivalence begins at the oral-sadistic state with the emergence of the teeth and the biting activity, becoming more frequent in the sadistic-anal phase. In this, the opposite pairs of impulses are already developed, but the subordination of these impulses aiming the reproduction will only occur in adult genital organization.

These opposite impulse pairs, the ambivalence between love and hate, are essential for understanding the doubt symptom. About the love-have ambivalence, Freud always reports:

> Love [...] almost does not distinguish hate in its attitude towards the object. Only after the genital organization establishment is that love becomes the opposite of hate [...]. Hate, as a relationship with the objects, is older than love. It results from the narcissistic ego primordial repudiation to the outside world [...]. Love so often manifests as 'ambivalent'- i.e., accompanied by impulses of hate against the same object (1915, p. 143).

In the adult genital organization, conscious love reaches a high degree of intensity in a way to be sufficiently strong to keep under repression its opponent. Love cannot annul hate, but only repress it in the unconscious system. And hate, in the unconscious, protected from the threat of being destroyed by the conscious operations, can persist and, even, to grow. This same hate can be reinforced by a regression from love to sadistic phase, because of love intensity directed towards the same object hides a hate of equal or greater intensity.

Discussion

Analyzing the excerpt taken from a clinical case with the problematic that he proposes to discuss, we can point out that the doubts presented by Paulo are related to love-hate ambivalence as a result of the libido fixation in his early childhood. I state this based on the transference relationship; since what is at stake is the paternal complex internalized at an early childhood of this patient; and, the movements of retaining associations (of not symbolically giving the faeces to the analyst when this patient is more contained) or to freely associate it when not suffering of trapped gases; as he himself said. I notice that when this patient is more 'relaxed' and less 'contained', he can capture better the psychotherapeutic interventions, replying: "I fully agree with you doctor [...]". But, in most of my interventions, when he is more contained, full of hate, he always replies: "I am going to disagree with you, I do not think that [...]" Thus, the giving and retaining faeces is manifested, in a symbolic way, expelling the associations or in the understanding (or not) of the interventions. Here comes the doubt as a symptomatic formation against the most primitive hate for the father figure embodied in the figure of the analyst. And it is this hate that moves this patient doubts against his progress under analysis. So, the doubt still is the ultimate resistance weapon of this patient.

The ruminant doubts also highlight the relationship of master and slave in this patient. When he is less contained, he behaves as a son submissive to the father; but when he is more contained, he puts himself in a relation of tremendous revolt, complaining about the injustices of his authoritarian boss. I notice that in the relationship with this boss, his sense of justice is a never-ending revolt, fed by his ambivalence. Currently he is suing the company, since they reduced his salary. Therefore, all his revolt acts are demonstrated in this 'hate' related to his intestinal gases since childhood.

The fact of giving or not the faeces to the analyst is also related to the paternal sadist penis that left this patient handed over the homosexuality ghost. When expelling the memories in his associations, the equation faeces-penis works as a pleasant movement, referring to the former anal eroticism of passive pleasure with the father figure, and which ramifications are currently related to the pleasure that he feels about smells and odors. On the other hand, while retaining the associations, this act expresses the old childish sadism, symbolically manifested by hate in containing the father's faeces, denoting the activity relationship with the external environment. Thus, the activity-passivity relations are manifested by providing or not the association, the faeces, to the psychotherapist.

In addition, I notice that he presents a rigid superego. This inflexibility perpetuates his doubts. And from my observation I began to ease this superego and sew it. So, I was relieving the rigidity of this instance and, therefore, as he himself said, the gases began to loosen. In this 'loosening' the doubts emerged in the therapeutic setting. These doubts, which were already part of Paulo's life story since the age of seven, are the resistance weapons of his own self in favor of the transfer; since they denote the ambivalence of love-hate in the transference relationship with the analyst. On the other hand, this ambivalence denotes the identification with the father figure permeated with unconscious hate; since this patient walked parallel paths to the paternal ways; but which is currently present in the infantile sadism ramifications that are manifested in the fact of promoting family meetings to reach collective decisions; because if someone requests an indi-

vidual decision, that causes him much embarrassment. Therefore, the fact of promoting family meetings and exercising the
control over his sons puts in evidence the unconscious sadistic
aspects of this patient.

Conclusion

From the excerpt analyzed above, I might point out that
the doubt symptomatic formation of patient Paulo evidences
all the unconscious hate against the father figure, and this hate
is manifested in the transfer with the analyst figure. The ambivalence between the love towards the father, such as the hate
related to him and repressed in his early childhood, serves as a
propelling spring of this symptom, feeding this patient resistance; also, favoring (or not) his free associations. Therefore, any
study of this symptom, in this class of neurosis, necessarily must
consider the ambivalent manifestations of anal-sadistic phase;
because it is in this one that we find the ambivalent impulses
(of love and hate, of activity and passivity) related to external
objects, fomenting these patients' uncertainties.

Bibliographical References

FENICHEL, O. (1981). *Psychoanalytic Theory of Neurosis.*São
Paulo: Livraria Atheneu.
FREUD, Sigmund (1905/1996). *Three essays on the sexuality
theory. ESB*, vol.VII.
_____. (1913/1996). *The inclination to obsessional neurosis – a
contribution to the problem of the neurosis choice. ESB*, vol. X.
_____.(1915/1996). *The instincts and its Vicissitudes.ESB*, vol.
XIV, Rio de Janeiro: Imago.

_____. (1915/1996). *Repression.ESB*, vol. XIV, Rio de Janeiro: Imago.

_____. (1917/1996). *The instinct transformations exemplified in anal eroticism.ESB,* vol. XVII.

_____. (1918/1996). *History of an infantile neurosis.ESB*, vol. XVII.

_____. (1933/1996). *Conference XXXII – Anxiety and instinctive life.ESB,* vol. XXII, 1996.

_____. (1937/1996). *Constructions in Analysis.ESB*, vol. XXIII. Rio de Janeiro: Imago.

PONTALIS; J. B. (2002). *Journal of Psychoanalysis.*São Paulo.

PONTALIS; J. B; LAPLANCHE, J. (2001/2004). Vocabulary of Psychoanalysis. São Paulo: Martins Fontes.

RIBEIRO, Maria Anita Carneiro Ribeiro (2003). *The ObsessionalNeurosis.* Rio de Janeiro: Jorge Zahar.

The Institutional Psychology in a prison unit: a brief report

Introduction

This paper aims to perform a brief analysis of the institutional psychologist inserted into a prison re-socialization unit, a context in which the supervision of learning groups aimed at the professional training of its in-patients was carried out.

The adopted methodology was the qualitative in which a theoretical-practical articulation is established from the works of Bleger, Baremblitt, Rouchy, Kaes, among others. Therefore, as the analysis field is analyzed, the verbalizations and complaints that occur during the professional qualification courses of a single group with about 20 members, in which the institutional psychologist role came to act as a filter for the in-patients that clamored for a listener, extrapolating the institutional walls.

Results

These groups were formed from a demand diagnosis, in which, theoretically, the students were chosen due to their low professional qualification. In practice, many were chosen from the good behavior in the institution. These groups were pre-formed by the choices from their own internal directors and the institutional psychologist was 'contacted' to carry out the proper educational supervisions during its progress.

As the analysis demand emerged from an 'analysis device' surrounded by conflicts between what was instituted and the values of some instituting individuals, every visit was pre-scheduled, being the time and duration pre-determined, thus avoiding possible future conflicts. As the analysis field, only one group was chosen, in which it was possible to find a richness in plurality that enriched the understanding of this institution movements.

Therefore, as the demand is constituted by the offer, this paper analyzes how this institution is molded and adapted to this group of in-patients' desires, reinventing some paradigmatic values.

Institutional Psychology

In his article, *Institutional Psychology*, Bleger (1992) points out that "the institutional psychology [...]is a recent chapter in the Psychology development and nobody can, currently, exhibit or lean on an extensive experience" (p. 32). In psychology still predominates this clinical inheritance, although currently the psychologists are not in only one psychotherapeutic activity, but they are also performing with a clinical-social approach, including its corresponding conceptual model and increasing the scope in which they work. Therefore, the institutional psychology is inserted in the history of social needs, being the empirical research of utmost relevance for its progress.

And it was in this research need that I observed the movement of this training group within the unit under study, emphasizing the interaction sociability levels and the syncretic sociability levels.

At the beginning of this group formation, when the first supervisions were carried out, the syncretic sociability predominated. This means that these people seemed to be in a "fusion or indiscrimination state" (Bleger, 2011, p. 107). Thus, the silence showed the paranoid reactions due to the fear for new experience and the unknown and, as Bleger (2011) says, "it is not only the new that produces fear, but rather the unknown that exists within the known" (p. 110).

During the other visits, I noticed that this group began to develop a syncretic group identity. For Bleger (2011), this identity "lies in its belonging to the group" (p.112). Such observation arises from the interactions that began to emerge from the second week, when many complaints came from the students belonging to this group, as it occurred regarding the quality of the snack offered. That is, during this course, this group would have the right to a snack, but this, sometimes, was not enough for everyone. At this point, the individual barrier was broken and a 'primary' collective began to form, claiming the snack improvement during the supervisions.

When listening to these complaints, I understood that they pointed to a greater degree of belonging to the group, in which its members were seeking a greater identity for integration. Therefore, the members of this training group tended to syncretic sociability, where the preverbal behaviors became common. With the teacher, they hardly complained, but when I visited them, some presented complaints of this institution movements. Consequently, many students demonstrated their resistance movements, missing classes, verbally attacking teachers and other colleagues. So, at this moment, the institution showed the latent movements.

But what would be the institution? Bleger (2011) understands the institution as "a set of rules and standards and activities groups around values and social functions" (p.114). The group can be considered as an institution, but if it is stabilized, this can turn into an anti-therapeutic group and, if it is bureaucratized, its means will become the purposes, losing its objectives.

In addition, it is convenient to highlight that the institutional psychology involves the "conceptual models reform and the expansion of the work scope" (Bleger, 1992, p. 34). The institutional psychology would not be a field of applied psychology, but a research field of the social reality phenomena. Within this, Bleger highlights the task classification and the resources administration.

For Bleger (1992) "the institutional psychology comprises [...]a set of organisms of concrete physical existence, which have a certain degree of permanence in a field [...]to study in it all human phenomena" (p. 37). These human phenomena, in the focused unit, despoiled the boycott movements along the laws enforcement. These 'boycotts' departed from the macro level (institution) to the meso level (learning group) and vice versa. At this point, many students assumed the role of scapegoat, reinventing and violating some rules.

And when taking care of just one group, I could capture how this occupied an entire singular dynamic. Although the diagnosis was 'premolded' by the own director, I observed the singular movements in this group, being my interventions the result of these observations in which the mental models of this unit managers was not always reiterated.

When achieving a unique vision, I sought to analyze the latent contents of the unconscious movements of this institution, in which the instituting individuals manifested that the group identity became a group that not always accomplished what was established, emerging the interest conflicts as a form of latent contents manifestation, being these contents feedback of utmost relevance to this prison unit maturity.

These were the "urgency points" (Bleger, 1992, p. 45), as a result of these conflicts, that I sought to understand and analyze so that, subsequently, the appropriate interventions were carried out. In these interventions, the key point was to understand the resistance movement of both sides: if, on one hand, there were employees who did not accept the public policies for the in-patients and, on the other side, the in-patients did not accept the institution educational impositions. In order to ease these conflicts, I sat with the in-patients in their corresponding class-rooms, listened to them, interlacing and understanding their individual historicity with the institutional movement. From this, I listed a diagnosis for each visit, carrying out the necessary interventions 'in loco', with the directors, in a first movement, and with the in-patients of this group, in a second moment.

This investigation enabled the task development and the future classification of each situation itself. For this purpose, the use of the clinical method was of utmost relevance for the task, since, within this, the psychologist is guided "by the classification systematic introduced by the psychoanalytic technique, adapted to the needs of this scope" (Bleger, 1992, p. 46). Thus, the detailed observation of internal movements was of utmost relevance for the task closure, leading to the classification of these conditions through the observation.

In this prison unit, from the classifications, my actuation allowed the understanding of existing problems, being these explicit through the courses operability. It was the operationality, or its lack, which was also evident in this institution conflicts and, consequently, of the group under study.

According to Bleger (1992), the institutional conflict is of utmost importance to its growth. In his wise words, "the best 'degree of dynamics' of an institution is not given by the absence of conflicts, but rather by the possibility to explain them, manage them, and solve them within the institutional limit" (Bleger, 1992, p. 52). Throughout the course, many denied the conflicts authorship, demonstrating certain scission of their own personality, thus hindering the task. During my interventions, I always pointed out the importance of assuming these conflicts and verbalizing it to the group, although many did not see the conflict as beneficial. Therefore, all intervention techniques were by and through the group, although the practice demonstrated the lack of group cohesion due to the persecution anxieties of its members.

From the Institutional Psychology to the Institutional Analysis.

As the discussion was highlighted, from the encounter of these 'instituting' analyses, many enjoyed the narcissistic benefits of this institution, strengthening the narcissistic contract of each of these members with the group, reiterating the denegation pact. This pact denoted the conflict between the instituted and the instituting individuals, leading them to a sense of alienation and standstill.

If from one hand, we have the instituting individuals moved by the productive forces of institutional logics, on the other, we have the instituted, in which we find a system that cannot re-socialize its in-patient and, in the absence of its ability, heavily invests in educational courses.

For Rouchy and Desroche (2005) "the structures internalized by the establishment members are part of the psychic reality and the values; and they determine [...]the group organization mode, the usual relations and the interaction networks" (p.68). It was in these interaction networks that the conflicts emerged, because there was a veiled pact that only the "good" in-patients could participate in these courses. And it was from this maneuver that the complaints present in this institution demand, highlighting how the formal groups – the socio-educational teams – established the informal groups of in-patients, requiring various interventions in the micro level.

And it was from these in-patients' narratives encounter that this study highlights some peculiarities for the development of this analysis, such as the "narcissistic benefits" (Kaes, 1988, p. 5). This means that many in-patients enjoyed the benefits and privileges to continue "binding" into his institutional roots, not aspiring anything different for his future and reinforcing, therefore the narcissistic contract of each of these members with this re-socialization institution.

Kaes (1988) also points out that "when the institution does not support the narcissism of its members [...], the institution is attacked" (p.26). This quote matches with the conflicts demands that emerged due to certain cuts of benefits of some instituting individuals, leading them to feel devaluated by the institution. And in the absence of frustrations elaborations, these went to violence with other in-patients, repeating the possible tension between the filiation and affiliation of his primary group. Therefore, such as the family that has not invested love and attention, they charged the institution for the lack of these, as if it was guilty for their violence and delinquency acts. Consequently, when completing this reeducation course and leaving this unit, many showed a very unusual movement: they took from society what supposedly this deprived them: the love and attention, thus building a vicious circle of several exits and returns to it.

In addition, it was from the instituted that emerged the suffering of these in-patients, leading them to a sense of alienation. About this, Kaes (1988) states: "it is against the emergence of this repressed and against the recognition of this unconscious [...] that the own defenses of institutional existence are established" (p. 29). He observed that it was in these defenses that the instituting suffering denoted the precarious operation of this institution.

Still according to Kaes (1988), "the institutions are continually deconsecrated and consecrated" (p. 04). This re-socialization institution, besides bringing narcissistic benefits to the individual unconscious of each in-patient, it also featured narcissistic benefits for the society in which it was inserted, fostering the moral judgments for its external, enjoying and feeding its own perverse desire, so denoting the "denegation pact" (Kaesapud Brandt, 2007, p. 03), in other words, something that could never be exposed. This pact comes to give support to the narcissistic contract, since the training courses were accepted under only one condition: if they were offered for the in-patients' benefits, and for the employees, bonuses for the goals reached.

Conclusion

This paper concludes that the learning group studied would require a greater cohesion, being the demand for analysis arising from its internal interactions and not as a result of educational policies that did not aim the internal growth of its members, and the valuation of the instituted, in pursuit of those that did not fit in these rules and reinforcing the in-patients' persecutory anxieties, causing the non-cohesion of the group and the boycott movements to institutional rules.

In addition, the denegation pact reinforced the unconscious alliance between the employees and in-patients, denoting the set of forces present in the instituting individuals regarding what was already established, making the benefits resulting from these courses a defense of the instituted that imprisoned them against future changes. These social benefits supported this pact, revealing the set of forces that could not be verbalized, but which were tacit in the narcissist contract.

Bibliographical References.

BLEGER, J. (2011). *Psychology topics: interview and groups.* Translation Rita Maria M. de Moraes.4ᵗʰEdition.SãoPaulo:Martins Fontes. (Original published in 1980).

BLEGER, J.(1992). *Psycho-hygiene and institutional psychology.* Translation of Emilia de Oliveira.Porto Alegre:Artes Médicas.

BLEGER, J.(1975). *Psychoanalysis of the Psychoanalytic Frame.* Buenos Aires: Paidós.(Original published in 1967).

DELEUZE, G. (1996). *The mystery of Ariana.* Lisbon:Ed.Vega – Passagens.

KAËS, R. (1988). Psychic reality and suffering in institutions.

In:KAËS, R.; BLEGER, J.; ENRIQUEZ, E.; FORNARI, F.; FUSTIER, P.; ROUSSILLON, R.; VIDAL, J. P. (Orgs.).*The institution and the institutions.*Translation.J. P. Neto.SãoPaulo:Casa do Psicólogo.

Lewin, K. (1978). *Field Theory in Social Science.* Buenos Aires: Paidós.

ROUCHY, J. C. & DESROCHE, M. S. (2005). *Institution and Change: psychic process and organization.*SãoPaulo:Casa do Psicólogo.

Symbols of Transformation: preludes analysis of a schizophrenia

(summary of volume 05, of Carl Gustav Jung book)

The summary of this book aims to highlight the main points of this rich work that demarcates the rupture between Freud and Jung. If, on the side of Psychoanalysis, we have the book *Totem and Taboo*, as a response to the questions of Jung, on the side of the newly founded Analytical Psychology, we have this milestone, the book *The Symbols of Transformation*, representing the rupture between these two geniuses.

For understanding it, nothing better than a panorama of its main passages. I remind that Jung wrote three prefaces for this book, once the preparation and modifications within this stretched for nearly 40 years, throughout his life.

This book was written when Jung was 36 years old, time of his breakup with Freud. In 1911, Jung wrote it up to chapter V, entitled *The Song of the Moth* and, from 1912, continued to the second complete part, concluding it. Therefore, this summary is based on the definitive edition of 1952, in which the terminology of the period psychoanalysis was abandoned, a time in which Jung starts using the very terms of Analytical Psychology, such as the major archetypal manifestations – the anima-animus, shadow and selves.

The first milestone of this book is the new understanding of libido, in which this would be a psychic energy directed rather than a manifestation of pure sexuality, questioning, thus, Freud's psychoanalytic theory and its individualistic model. On the other hand, he brings the role of myth. It would be through this that the patient would contact his past and the lives of his ancestors. At this point, he interweaves a differentiation between the individual consciousness and the individual unconscious, exemplifying that the consciousness would only be the blooming and the fruiting characteristic of the season, evolving from the perennial underground rhizome that would be the roots of the universal mother originating in the collective unconscious. Therefore, the entire empirical, clinical material in this book has its roots in the collective unconscious, being the mutable psyche, a fruit of its history on the march and in which religion comes to play a role of utmost relevance, especially in the creation of symbols on the interface between the consciousness and the unconscious. Thus, the religious ground comes to provide a bridge, where the symbols are built and 'resignified'.

This book is based on the analysis of the mental historical facts which meet in an involuntary individual fantasy. This fantasy would be the 'creating' fantasy which refers to the forgotten primitive spirit, backing into its peculiar images that are revealed in the mythologies of all times and of all people. For Jung (1912), the set of these images form the collective unconscious, present in all individuals by heredity. These images are subject to reappear spontaneously everywhere. This fact justifies why the temporal and more distanced mythologem may belong to the same creator base: the human psyche, since the brain, despite the small variations, works everywhere in the same way.

This book exalts the case of Miss Miller, a patient who showed her unusual capacity for empathy and identification, although his examples of suggestibility were quite rich. While bringing the associations of Miller, Jung emphasizes the self-suggestibility effect, a moment when the libido has taken certain impressions and exaggerated it "due to the presence of the free energy 'available' as a result of an insufficient relationship with reality" (Jung, 1912, p. 59). The rich case of this patient showed the difficulty of a real affective relationship, leading it to strengthen her almost magical influence over another person, highlighting the suggestion strength present in her fantasies. This would exemplify the self-suggestibility, which action comes to exemplify how the libido has taken certain impressions and exaggerated it, thanks to the presence of the free energy available as a result of a bad relationship with reality.

Jung continues with this clinical case in item IV entitled *The Hymn of Creation*, bringing, early, the issue of 'dementia parecox', i.e. schizophrenia. He frames a critique to the psychiatry of this time, although he highlights the consequences of reality introversion, a fact that manifested in the patient Miss Miller. He understands the schizophrenia as a mental disorder in which patients are increasingly closed against reality, submerging in their fantasies as the external reality weakness its influence and the inner world increases its authoritative strength.

Another important contribution is that Jung (1912) elaborates a conceptualization of the term imago. This would be the live independence in the psychic hierarchy, an autonomy "that crystallized as an essential particularity of the feelings complex at the expense of multiple experiences" (1912, p. 65). He also highlights that, throughout his work, he came to use the term archetype to treat the impersonal and collective reasons. For this author, archetype would be the structures where we find an innate predisposition for creating parallel fantasies, of "identical, universal structures of psyche" (1912, p. 190) and which he designated, afterwards, as collective unconscious.

It would be in this unconscious where the archetypes are present, where the patient is driven by instinct, due to his limitation or inhibition, to a possible regression, animating these archetypal structures.

Here there is an interesting data: libido loses the sexual character conceived by Freud, becoming a driving force of the soul and which essence would yield 'useful and harmful, good and bad things' (1912, p. 150). And why this new conception is so important to Jung? Because the creation of symbols is closely linked to the libido. For Jung "we cannot treat the formation

Henrique Guilherme Scatolin

of symbols without including the instinctive processes, because from these come the driving force of the symbol" (1912, p. 273). Therefore, most of the symbols, to a greater or lesser extent, presents analogies of sexuality instinct, moment when the libido would fill the archetypes, "universally present and inherited forms that, in its totality, constitute the structure of the unconscious" (1912, p. 273). Thus, the archetypes are forms or beds into which the rivers of psychic phenomena would flow forever.

In addition, Jung (1912) understands that sexuality plays an important role in the formation of symbols, especially the religious. He points out how the first Christians would have distanced so strongly of their instincts, avoiding contact with their own sexuality, this would have provoked symbolic marks in Christianity, propitiating the formation of spiritual images. Thus, the symbols would offer paths for the libido, making them as bridges for the greatest achievements of humanity. These would have as a base the unconscious archetype, and which apparent image comes from the ideas that the conscious acquired.

Jung considers the archetypes "as structural elements [...] of psyche" (1912, p. 277). It has autonomy and specific energy, in which the symbols would be its transformers, because they would lead to a lower sphere libido - of collective unconscious - to a higher form. The symbol would act in a suggestive manner, expressing the conviction contents. Jung mentions numerous symbols in this book, but I would like to mention a few:

- The symbol of the tree: this is a maternal symbol, leading to religious myths;
- The symbol of the serpent: this would have a phallic significance and in the religious myths, in contrast to orgy and the manifestation of sexuality, this would have a "religious connotation" (1912, p. 443). He points out that in the Ophites mysteries, the solemnity was celebrated with snakes and some animals were even kissed.

But how would the symbols transformations occur? For Jung (1912), the man is just transformed into what is already potentially inside him. Each transformation is unconsciously compensated by the archetype through another form of adaptation and signification, such as the cross can represent the removal of all misery, but also a symbol of rain and fertility. Thus, the cross is a symbol of many meanings, being one of its main meaning the life tree and the mother.

And so that the symbols break out, Jung (1912) mentions the regression. This would seek the path of libido so that the symbols break out as an expression, not allowing, in some cases, that libido stays stuck on maternal materiality. In every regression, libido can be diverted to a symbol or an equivalent symbolic of the father or the mother, in the collective unconscious. And, in addition to the regression, we would have the introversion of libido as another fundamental mechanism in the creation of symbols. So, coming back to the serpent symbol.

For Jung, the unconscious can insinuate in the form of a serpent when the conscious fear the rewarding trend of the unconscious, which usually occurs in the regression; but who assumes an affirmative attitude towards the compensation does not regress and "will go" towards the unconscious through introversion" (1912, p. 446). In many historical examples, it is through introversion that the individual is fertilized, delighted, re-generated and reborn.

Jung (1912) weaves another criticism to Freudian psychoanalysis, because in the 'incest barrier' pointed by Freud there is a sexualist allegorizing. For Jung (1912) not everything is reduced to sexual pleasure, since "pleasure can be present in multiple sources" (1912, o. 487). He points out that the incest barrier " is a very dubious barrier (no matter how good it is for describing the neurotic states), since it represents a cultural acquisition that was not invented, but naturally originated, based on complicated biological needs that related to the appearance of the so-called marriage class systems" (1912, p. 487). These systems are not aimed at the prevention of incest, but rather the social danger of endogamy, a moment in which marriage would not prevent incest, very frequent in promiscuity attacks of primitives, but it would assume the need to extend the social organization to the entire tribe. It was not the incest taboo that removed the man from the indiscrimination state, but rather his *development instinct* and this imposed several taboos, differentiating him from other animals. In this context, he resumes the neurosis that, in his understanding, is not focused on the sexual theory and rather to the regression to the oral via, resplending the fear of being swallowed, denoting the act of being devoured. In this meander, the Oedipus complex is transformed into the Jonas-whale context, where the fear of incest becomes the fear of being eaten by the mother. The regression of libido is unsexed and, in the myth of Jonas and the whale, this regresses to the collective psyche where Jonas sees the mysteries, the collective representations, inside the whale belly. Therefore the libido regression can animate collective images, the archetypes, which will have a rewarding and healing meaning, as the myth has always had.

Jung points out that libido "in regression is hidden in numerous and quite variable symbols, regardless of male or female nature" (1912, p. 499). Libido can be an unstoppable impulse forward, in search of living and building; but it can also search its decline, its involution (a contradiction that is exemplified by the Verona statuette). So, the more the conscious denies the modification, more the symbols will perpetuate in dreams and premonitions, becoming scary symbols. For example, the serpent, as a symbol of fear, can represent a precedence of physical illness, but the interpretation will depend on the individual circumstances of each patient.

In the epilogue, Jung brings the conclusion of Miss Miller case, since this case represents a clinic of unconscious manifestations. He points out that fantasies "come from a psychic energy not subject to the conscious control" (1912, p. 513). In these fantasies we find impulses and symbolic events unrelated to the conscious. If the analyst explained the meaning of these fantasies to the patient, this would avoid the danger of his dissociations and which assimilation would avoid the isolation and, consequently, the psychosis.

It is in the gaps between the conscious and the unconscious that we can observe the neurosis and psychosis. In the individual with the tendency to neurosis, in this gap, we could find a neurotic state and in the individual with predisposition to psychosis, this gap could lead to isolation and schizophrenia, causing isolation and panic. The role of therapy, in both pathological frames, would lead to the integration of unconscious to consciousness contents, decreasing the dissociation. However, when the unconscious impulses are made instinctively, the spiritual contents are not taken into consideration. For this reason, the symbol comes to play a very important role, allowing the crossing between both sides. Therefore, the archetypal relations of unconscious products only occur with the collective representations, since the collective contents would be present in the transfer and are exalted in dreams, visions, fantasies and manias.

Summary concluded in the city of Brotas – SP, on
January 17th, 2015.

Bibliographical Reference

JUNG, C. G (2011). *Symbols of transformation: preludes analysis of a schizophrenia.* Translation of Eva Estern. 7th ed. Petrópolis: Vozes. Original published in 1912.

The Institutional Unconscious (the book review)

The Institutional Unconscious

This book is the result of the reformulated minutes of the II International Symposium of Psychoanalysis, Groups and Institutions that occurred at the beginning of the 80s in the city of Rio de Janeiro.

In the introduction, Baremblitt brings some features of the institutionalist movement, alerting the reader to its conceptual genesis in which there is a historical and dialectical materialism, occurring criticisms to the production modes, the State role and the family. Therefore, this movement was developed "as the unofficial option within the state capitalism, of various social democracies, of transition systems and the socialism [...]" (1982, p. 19). It behooved the institutionalists to criticize the most extensive explanations, since they did not aim to explain complex and concrete social situations, such as the production means. Consequently, they would develop singular resources to understand and intervene in each group.

Baremblitt brings 04 roundtables. At the first table, titled *Current Status of Individual and Group Psychoanalysis*, the coordinator, Luis Fernando de Mello Campos, and the participants Gregório Baremblitt, Armando Bauleo, Eduardo Pavlovsky and Osvaldo Saidon are present.

Bauleo brings the discussion on group psychoanalysis, in which he points the psychoanalysis in group and the psychoanalysis of the group. While in the psychoanalysis in group there is a search for the understanding of individuals isolated in a group, in the psychoanalysis of the group there is a search for the group psychoanalytic understanding.

At this point, Pavlovsky makes a historical resume in the group psychoanalysis history, making a serious criticism to the Bion theory of groups. He brings the self-management system, a system in which the supervision was precarious in its beginning, as he says: "We were not looking for a supervisor because we trusted that someone who did not do group psychotherapy came to teach us how to do group psychology" (1982, p. 30). One way was to adopt dramatic techniques. Therefore, he points out that the group psychotherapy is a practice that enables and requires the theorization in terms of a social-historical unconscious interlaced with the forces and work-related representations, to power and money.

The participant Saidon reiterates the criticism to Bion, making a criticism to the classic exercise of individual psychoanalysis, resuming the criticisms of Besaglia to the orthodox psychoanalysis and highlighting the influences of the institutionalist currents and of democratic psychiatry in Brazil. Bauleo reiterates the wise criticism of Saidon, since, when it comes to group structure, he emphasizes that it is necessary to insist that it is organized due to the differences between the subjects.

Finally, in the institutional field, Lourau differentiates the analysis field and the intervention field. While in the analysis field there is a grouping of materials and the production of knowledge about a particular conjuncture, in the intervention field there is the deployment of a concrete operating device enabling a generalized collective analysis. So, the intervention field is a "polymorphic and heterogeneous device intended to deconstruct the established and promote new unusual articulations" (1982, p. 56).

At the second table titled *Current Panorama of the Institutional Movement* are the coordinator Heliana Conde and the participants Gregório Baremblitt, Gérad Mendel, René Lourau, and J. A. Guilhon de Albuquerque. They discussed the institutionalist movement, resuming the political issues and emphasizing the institutional analysis characteristics. Lourau brings the beginning of investigations in the educational area, emphasizing the psycho-sociological model inspired in the American groups' dynamics and stressing the self-management and the analyzer concepts, as he says: "the self-management is very important in the socio-analytic intervention mechanism, since it refers to the performance of the entire operation, both its demand and the socio-analysts' fees payment" (1982, p. 76).So the analyzer would bring the analysis resolution, and before the intervention the order and the demand would arise. The order would be the result of the institutional power, emerging before the intervention. And the demand would occur along the interventions, connected to the social classes and their struggles.

Baremblitt resumes the word, highlighting the IBRAPSI (Brazilian Institute of Psychoanalysis, Groups and Institutions) value, pointing out that the institutional analysts' need to encompass a growing number of the population through institutional interventions.

At the roundtable number III, Osvaldo Saidon and the participants Gregório Baremblitt, Armando Bauleo, René Loureau, Gérad Mendel and Alejandro Scherzer were present. In this table, they emphasized the "critical-productive articulations between the individual, group and institutional interventions" (1982, p.99). The coordinator opens this table, stating that all analysis need "to include the group institutional dimension both from the instituted and from the instituting perspectives" (1982, p. 99). So, the group must be studied in its heterogeneity and its openness, and cannot be considered a homogenous and totalizing structure. The group needs to be a tactical space where one can see the unique, unusual and creative effects production, being its production and repetition (or stereotypy) an alternative for it.

These statements are completed by Professor Alejandro Scherzer who brings his experience with coupes, therapeutic groups and operating groups. He understands the group as "a set of people, who meet for a certain time, in a certain place, in a social context, to perform multiple tasks [...]. The group is an organization in which numerous institutions are corporified" (1982, p. 101-102). So, the group would be a space of institutional interweaving, in which we have political, economic and ideological determinations of the social set.

Upon returning the word to Mendel, this researcher stresses that the institutional analysis must be concerned with institutional relations in which the groups and its various collectivities are constituted. The groups could produce the regression phenomena among its members, in which the policy analysis can come from a kind of complicity that is "not conscious between the coordinator and the members of his group" (1982, p. 109).

This speech continues in table IV, in which is titled *Current Status of Psychiatry Institution and the Psychiatric Establishments*. This table includes the coordinator, Baremblitt, and the participants Armando Bauleo, José Augusto Guilhon de Albuquerque, Osvaldo Saindon, Alejandro Scherzer and Luis Fernando de Mello Campos.

In this table, Baremblitt introduces the exodus of the Jewish people to approach the institutions. Guilhon resumes the word, emphasizing that the institutional object "constitutes in the fabric, in the network of this and other existing institutions that determine it" (1982, p. 138). In this object, there is the legitimating discourse of institutional practices, being mentioned as an example, the electroshock therapy used in the 50s in psychiatric institutions.

If, on one hand, Mendel points out the regression in the group, on the other, Campos defines some aspects of the institution, ensuring that this is defined by the practices developed and the articulation between them. Therefore, the way in which the institution defines its object and its legitimating discourse is of utmost importance for its effectiveness.

At this point, Saidon resumes the word, highlighting his experiences in psychiatric hospitals and emphasizing the denunciation instruments that many use from the therapeutic groups in these hospitals. He interprets that it denounces the precariousness of transfer analysis due to the lack of commitment of some institutional analysts.

Bauleo, another participant in this table, resumes the law 180 promulgated in Italy aiming the abolition of asylums. This opening, according to this author, would be "as an end and a beginning in the psychiatry history" (1982, p. 149). This opening, according to the participants, should be complemented as a movement that goes to the community to create in it conditions to recycle and innovate the process within the institutions.

This table ends criticizing the Argentinean and European bourgeoisie, portraying that the social exclusion is also a result of the system and the order imposed by the State. For this purpose, he uses a beautiful metaphor: "it seems ridiculous to believe that a small puff can drill into a wall. But [...] it was the wind that made the mountains emerged. One should have the patience of the winds and blow them all at the same time. Men are generally less hard than the stones" (1982, p. 162).

Bibliographical Reference

Baremblitt, G. F. (1982). *The Institutional Unconscious*. Petropolis: Vozes.

The Brazilian Psychiatric Reform

The Brazilian Psychiatric Reform

This work aims to point out Franco Basaglia influences, of Italian Democratic Psychiatry, for the psychiatric hospitals deinstitutionalization phenomenon in the Brazilian territory.

The psychiatric reform movement in Brazil assumed different models in each Brazilian state. According to Pacheco (2009), the psychiatric reform in our territory suffered a strong influence of European experiences, specifically from the Italian reform and the thought that restricted it, and was, slowly, adapting to the particularities of each region in the country. Still according to Pacheco (apud Lobosque, 1997), the singularity, limit and articulation principles shaped the reform in Brazil.

The singularity principle represents "an invitation to the individual for maintaining his particularity and difference, appropriating and respecting the culture limits" (Pacheco, 2009, p.143). This principle would lead society to coexist with differences, resulting in the extension of social limits. Concomitantly to this principle, the limit principle goes beyond the social rules internalization by the individual with psychic disorders, extending his limits and providing the society the possibility to deal with the various forms of difference. And the articulation principle is intended for the interdisciplinary character of field action and the mental health dialogue with other areas of knowledge, leading to a transformation of cultural values.

The great milestone of this reform was the creation, in 1978, of the National Mental Health Workers Movement, allowing new political, theoretical and technical reflections about psychiatric care. Still according to Pacheco "currently we can witness the development of psychiatric reform experiences throughout the national territory" (2009, p. 144). Although this movement takes a particularity in each region, this reform still faces two care models, causing many conflicts: the insane asylum that persists in the culture, in which the exclusion and madness alienation traces are still present, and on the other side, the anti-asylum clinics, seeking the reintegration of people with mental disorders and the right to human treatment, trying not to silence the symptom.

It is worth remembering that, before the Mental Health Workers Movement, the introduction of insane asylum model in Brazil had already suffered severe criticisms, such as by Nise de Silveira, who in 1955, called the attention to the psychiatric hospitals insufficiency. According to Pacheco, at this time, the psychiatric hospital was seen "as a care device [...] that promoted a vicious cycle and the constitution of a psychiatric career, which was impossible to leave" (2009, p. 145).

In his book, *Psychiatric Reform, a Possible Reality*, Pacheco (2009) also brings three periods preceding the reform in Brazil. The first period is dedicated to the therapeutic communities and the institutional psychotherapy, in which patients would have the right to participate in the decision-making within the institutions. Thus, according to Pacheco, in the post-World II period, the therapeutic communities and institutional psychotherapy can be considered reorganization strategies of psychiatric institutions.

The second period was supported "by a psychiatry extension to public space, directed to preventive actions and Mental Health promotion, considered in this context as a social adaptation process" (2009, p.125). If, on one hand, at this time, there were advances with the community aspect, on the other hand, the hospital-center model still predominated, in which the community services, in order to detect people with possible mental disorders, were still within psychiatric hospitals.

In the third period occurs the Anti-psychiatry and the Italian Democratic Psychiatry that broke with the previous paradigms, highlighting a new construction of subjectivity and modifying the madness concept as knowledge solely focused on medicine, posting a new understanding to it: madness would be a phenomenon among humans, the result of a social production. This would not justify excluding actions in its treatment.

In this period we have the name of Franco Basaglia who was noticed as a pioneer of the psychiatric reform.

Basaglia, in his book *Selected Writings,* makes a strong criticism to the way inmates were treated in the asylums early in the 20th century in Italy, pointing out the assistance tied to the fear, piety and security. This time, it fell to the doctor "the mere role of vigilant, internal tutor, moderator of the excesses to which the disease could lead [...]" (2010, p. 24). The institutionalized, in these conditions, corresponds to the motionless man, without notion of future, without changing interest, and destroyed by the institution power. Unlike the past, the Italian reform, with the insane asylums opening, produced a gradual transformation in its space, causing a new relation with mental disease. It would fall to psychiatrists to give voice to these patients, breaking the institutionalization caused by medications, seeking the patients' human re-education and reestablishing links with the outside world, in which they would also organize their life at the hospital according to their therapeutic community.

For Basaglia (2010) this opening gives the patient the perception of living in a treatment place where he can gradually regain his relationship with other people, creating a trust link with whom takes care of him and his companions. And to avoid the bland institutionalization, in which the patient would later devote a gratitude for his freedom to an external act and not his, it would be the psychiatrist duty to create a new concept of psychiatric hospital, considering, firstly, the patient and a dimension suitable to him. In this space the therapeutic communities were included.

It would be in these communities that the patient would recover "the value and domain of himself, his place, and even his role in the hospital space, which walls are just the property limit" (Basaglia, 2010, p.33). Here the Day Hospital would be a point of union between the internal and external spaces, in which the patient would conquer his freedom gradually.

At this moment, in the 70's, the deinstitutionalization concepts gain strength. Although this concept is already in the European literature in the 30's, this concept is "relatively recent in the Brazilian academia" (Lougon, 2006, p. 142). And all modernization of mental disease care in Brazil, as well as in Latin America, has its roots in the transfer from central countries models. In Brazil, this modernization has suffered the influence of Italian Democratic Psychiatry, in the mid 80's, during the Psychiatric Reform second phase, although many authors (such as Delgado and Amarante) indicate this early in the 80's

This model came to criticize and denounce "the asylum care model based on hospital internment, as well as the private companies in the sector, called the 'madness industry' " (Lougon, 2006, p. 177). So, as a public strategy to reduce the beds in various hospitals, early in the 90's appears the PAD: Deinstitutionalization Support Program. This program aimed that inpatients for more than five years, or ten years with short discharge periods, could return to their origin families or to their substitute families.

In addition, Lougon highlights the sheltered homes, in which it would be another strategy "designed to insert ex-inpatients into the community [...]. These are houses or apartments financed with public funds, where they reside with the ex-inpatients who wish and have conditions to do so" (2006, p. 178).

In addition to the sheltered homes, I highlight that the deinstitutionalization process still stumbles in the various myths surrounding this movement. According to Lougon "there are segments that [...] involve the non-acceptance of former psychiatric patients by community, due to [...] prejudices and stigmas that involve the figure, sometimes unusual, of mental patients, generating rejection and distance" (2006, p.147). These myths and prejudices obstruct, often, these patients' integration with the environment that surrounds them, limiting the deinstitutionalization advances. And as an alternative to the hospitalization egresses, Brazil continues implementing the Psychosocial Care Centers (Caps), several Psychosocial Care Nucleus (Naps) and similar structures as alternative means to these hospitals.

Therefore, this work concludes that the Brazilian psychiatric reform brought transformations in the social and political spheres in this country, pointing to new discussions about the mental disease sphere, leading to a new representation of madness in a pursuit of their rights and duties.

Bibliographical References

BASAGLIA, F. (2010). *Selected Writings on Mental Health and the Psychiatric Reform.* Translation of Joana Angélica d'Ávila Melo. Rio de Janeiro: Garamond.

LOUGON, M. (2006). *Institutional Psychiatry: From the Asylum to the Psychiatric Reform.* Rio de Janeiro: Fiocruz.

PACHECO, J. G. (2009). *Psychiatric Reform, a possible reality::social representations of madness and the story of an experience.*Curitiba: Juruá.

SOARES, M. H.; BUENO, S. M. V. (2011). *Mental Health: new perspectives.* São Caetano do Sul:Yendis Ltda.

www.ingramcontent.com/pod-product-compliance
Lightning Source LLC
Chambersburg PA
CBHW032354280326
41935CB00008B/570